I0016678

COMPUTING, A PRÉCIS ON SYSTEMS, SOFTWARE AND HARDWARE

ISBN: 978-1-291-05102-5

Copyright © Andreas Sofroniou 2012

All rights reserved.

COMPUTING, A PRÉCIS ON SYSTEMS, SOFTWARE AND HARDWARE

2012 Copyright © Andreas Sofroniou

ISBN: 978-1-291-05102-5

CONTENTS:

INFORMATION PROCESSING

The world of computing got smaller in 1993 in terms of both new ultra-small computing systems and the downsizing of giant computer corporations. Yet for all its shrinkage, the computing industry also reached out in a big way. The new, small computers were equipped with wireless networking systems, and home and office computers were offered the promise of networking with other computers worldwide on a data superhighway.

Today, computing is affecting work and leisure alike, increasingly involved in factory and business operations, networking, defence, medicine, education and the domestic environment. Computers and their systems are influencing attitudes to privacy, employment and other social issues.

To this effect, the reader must remember that the construction of a system is as complex as a house built in a swamp. It does, therefore, require careful planning and design. Just as a house must have an architect's plan, so does a system. It must have requirements, system objectives and a blueprint.

COMPUTER BACKGROUND

The early electronic computers of the 1940s had central processing units built up of banks of vacuum tubes, 'the glass bottles', also found in old wireless sets and television receivers. The CPUs (Central Processing Units), needed thousands of these tubes. The systems were cumbersome and unreliable, only hours between failures. There were heavy electrical power demands and the cooling plant was often as large as the computer.

The first computer of this type was ENIAC (Electronic Numerical Integrator and Computer), developed in the USA by J P Eckert and JW Mauchmy. ENIAC completed by 1946 was designed with the purpose of generating artillery firing tables. Built up of 18,000 vacuum tubes; it was immense, requiring a room 60 feet by 25 feet to hold it and weighing more than 30 tons.

In 1948, a transistor was first demonstrated by William Shockley, John Bardeen and Walter Brattain, working in the Bell Telephone Laboratory, in the USA. Transistors could do virtually all the jobs of the then conventional vacuum tube valves, but required much less electrical power, generated very little heat and were much smaller. They were considerably more reliable and made possible the development of computers as effective functional devices in an increasingly wide range of applications.

The computers of the fifties and early sixties, individually used thousands of transistors. The various electronic components, transistors, resistors, capacitors and diodes were mounted on printed circuit cards or boards. Copper was selectively edged from phenolic or fibreglass base to leave electrical connections between holes in which the wires of the components were inserted. A typical five-inch square printed circuit card would contain about a dozen transistors and a hundred or so other components.

Each computer (now second generation) comprised several thousand printed circuit cards. The cards, regarded as modules, were slotted into frames and interconnected by means of back-wiring. A typical large computer would be built up from several dozen specific modules, each of them being used up to several times in each computer.

In the sixties, the semi-conductor makers created a whole new technology, making possible the development of third generation computers. Using a more sophisticated version of transistor fabrication technology, it was possible to manufacture dozens of transistors together on a single small silicon chip. In this way an electronic circuit previously comprising many separate inter-connected components, could be manufactured as a single integrated unit.

By the early seventies, the basic components, transistors, diodes, etc. were assembled in a ten micro-millimetre thick surface layer in a silicon wafer. The components were then connected by metal layer evaporated on to the silicon. Subsequent etching produced a required inter-connection. Several of the integrated circuits could be mounted on a printed circuit card which could carry all the circuitry necessary for a central processing unit and the associated computer elements.

In recent years, integrated circuits were manufactured with a complexity of around one thousand transistors. The first micro-processor, produced by Intel Corporation in 1971, was based on a single quarter of an inch silicon chip which carried the equivalent of 2,250 transistors, all the necessary CPU circuitry for a tiny computer. By 1976, chips of this size using LSI (Large Scale Integration) could carry more than 20,000 components. Looking into the early part of the next millennium, the chip fabrication will allow larger chips to be built using smaller technology.

When a computer CPU is one integrated circuit, or a small number of circuits, the CPU is called a micro-processor. A micro-processor used with other integrated components forms a micro-computer.

The latest introduction of Intel's Pentium range, Motorola's and other manufacturers' equivalent PC-based capacity and speed, together with the personal computers software such as the Microsoft hold users in amazement and difficulty in following the development in computing.

In general, all modern computers and Personal Computers (PCs) have similar architecture features, functional elements equivalent to those of a large mainframe. The PCs may vary in performance according to their storage capacity. However, these are encroaching on many application areas, formerly the exclusive province of the larger computers.

The cost of computer hardware fell during the late nineties and as anticipated the resident software were given free as part of the PC. Application software, in a packaged form and helpful in running commercial systems, will be of minimal cost.

Today, PCs are affecting work and leisure alike, increasingly involved in factory and business operations, networking, defence, medicine, education and the domestic environment. They are influencing attitudes to privacy, employment and other social issues.

TECHNOLOGY

This reaching out also occurred on the software level. One of the most popular programs for the IBM personal computer (PC) and its compatible machines was Lotus Development Corp.'s Notes, a new version of which was marketed in 1993. 'Notes' is a "groupware" product, allowing groups of employees on a network, for instance, to produce a report jointly. Windows for Workgroups, a version of the popular Windows software, also debuted during the year, and there were plans for groupware that would link people working in their homes.

Another popular new product of 1993 also promoted connections between PC users. Named for its designer - the personal computer memory card industry association - the PCMCIA card was about the size of a business card and about 10 times as thick. When inserted into a special slot in a pocket-size computer, such as the Hewlett-Packard 95LX, it provided the PC with special functions such as extra memory. With a small radio built into it, a pocket computer could communicate with other pocket PCs or with local area networks (LANs). A PCMCIA card for the latter function was announced during the year by Proxim, Inc.; the card's speed was 40 times slower than that of most LANs.

While pocket computers were not new in 1993, a new type of handheld PC was introduced. Called the personal digital assistant (PDA), this palm-size computer was notable for having no keyboard. Instead, users wrote on its plastic screen with a special pen, and software then converted the handwriting to type. PDAs were introduced in 1993 by AT&T, Tandy Corp., and Apple Computer Inc., which called its product the Newton.

One problem with these PDAs was that there was no standard pen-based operating system; therefore, they could not interchange software as could standard PCs. Another consideration was that, because they were battery-operated and inexpensive - Apple's Newton started at about $700 - they did not have the processing power needed to keep up with fast writers or to translate their writing with perfect accuracy. Still another hurdle for PDAs was that there was no way to route the messages they created through the nation's computer networks. However, a consortium called General Magic, which included Apple and Sony Corp., announced that it was developing the software needed to accomplish this.

The best way to send messages from a PDA or any portable computer is without connecting any wires at all. The few means available to do this were expensive, but during the year the U.S. Federal Communications Commission (FCC) created "personal communications service," a cellular-like scheme having frequencies that could be used for wireless data links.

LINKUP OF NETWORKS

The planned fibre-optic network would not be the first offered by phone companies to improve data communications between homes and small businesses. In 1993 an integrated services digital network (ISDN) was being installed throughout the U.S. using the copper-wire network. ISDN allowed a home computer to send and receive information at rates 10 times faster than the fastest home computer modems and one consumer group claimed that it offered 80% of what fibre-optic networks would offer but at 10% of the cost. The telephone industry said its ISDN installations were going faster than expected and that by the end of 1994, 62% of lines would have the service, not the 55% it had expected by then.

Another existing computer network caught the public imagination in 1993. Non-commercial in nature and without any central management or, for the most part, funding, Internet was simply a linkup of diverse computer networks, most of them academic or research institutions. In 1993, however, publication after publication, including Harper's magazine, featured stories on the electronic mail (e-mail) sent back and forth in Internet's specialized forums - electronic bulletin boards that focused on everything from AIDS research to stamp collecting. One reason Internet was gaining popularity was that several software companies introduced programs in 1993 to make it easier to use, and several on-line information services opened gateways into this "network of networks."

As networking spread, it was likely to bring about changes in how the public thought about electronic versions of what was now received on paper. In what might someday be seen as a landmark case, a federal judge ruled during the year that e-mail generated by the U.S. president's office is as much a historical record as paper documents and cannot be erased when an administration changes.

BUSINESS

While connectivity was the major theme in computer hardware, the theme for the business of computers was continued upheaval. In fact, the year's biggest business story may have been the nearly $5 billion loss reported by IBM Corp., the largest corporate loss ever. In its aftermath, IBM's long time chairman, John Akers, was replaced by Louis Gerstner, Jr., the former chairman of RJR Nabisco. At Apple long time chairman John Sculley was replaced by Michael Spindler, the company's former chief of European operations, while Shigechika Takeuchi, president of Apple's Japanese subsidiary, resigned in November.

IBM's primary line of business was mainframe computers. From 1990 to 1992, however, its share of the world mainframe market dropped from 58% to 52%. IBM's 1993 financial statement revealed that the corporation's mainframe revenue had declined 12% and that all hardware sales were off 20%.

Another corporate crisis took place at NeXT Computer, Inc., a firm launched in 1985 by Apple cofounder Steve Jobs. Poor sales of its sole product, a workstation for education and engineering, caused the company to cease production and lay off about half of its 2,800 employees.

Also reporting a major loss was Borland International, Inc., once expected to be the third player in a PC software triumvirate with Microsoft Corp. and Lotus Development Corp. Borland experienced a third-quarter decline of $63 million and laid off 15% of its 2,200-employee workforce. It also began selling its financial analysis software for about $100, a fifth of the price of similar programs from Microsoft and Lotus.

Not every information-industry company shrank in 1993. AT&T decided to merge with the nation's largest independent cellular company, McCaw Cellular. And, in the largest U.S. communications merger ever, Bell Atlantic, a regional Bell telephone company, announced that it would buy cable television conglomerate TCI, Inc., which owned 1,200 local networks, for $21 billion. Bell Atlantic did not plan to operate the TCI networks within its own service area, but it would be allowed to use TCI lines outside its region to carry telephone calls. This would put it in competition with other "Baby Bells," a development the U.S. Department of Justice had not envisioned when it forced the break-up of AT&T in the early 1980s.

The proposed Bell Atlantic/TCI merger demonstrated how the computer and telecommunications businesses were merging. Cable TV by 1993 was capable of serving 95% of U.S. homes and businesses, and during the year it also became a medium for carrying corporate computer data, thanks to a new technology developed by Digital Equipment Corp.

As a result, cable TV companies could compete with telephone companies, which in turn wanted to get into the cable TV business in order to finance the laying of fibre-optic cable to homes. Unlike the copper-wire phone network, fibre-optic cable could carry movies and hundreds of television channels.

The Bell Atlantic/TCI merger would create the sort of "data superhighway" that the U.S. government was championing as a means to reduce costs in such industries as health care. According to one estimate, improved telecommunications would save the health-care industry $36 billion a year. Such a network could also be used to connect students with remote databases. The government wanted private industry to build the data superhighway, but it did plan to invest in research and development and to ease the market restrictions that might otherwise prevent a merger such as Bell Atlantic's.

Already the regulatory barriers were crumbling. In 1992 the FCC began allowing phone companies to carry information services such as dial-up versions of want ads, which a home computer could search in seconds by looking for key words.

SYSTEMS ENGINEERING

The reader must remember that the construction of a system is as complex as a house built in a swamp. It requires careful planning and design. Just as a house must have an architect's plan, so does a system. It must have requirements, system objectives and a blueprint.

In general, it must be well noticed that every system structured is an answer to the users' problems and requirements. The solutions will be based on the studies of the current systems, manual and computerised and the problems and requirements catalogue.

The design of the system will be based on how the users work and what suits the overall business environment. Whilst analysing the users' needs, the system engineer will proceed with the logical stages, by listening, interviewing and having Walkthroughs and reviews with users and colleagues.

Prior to proceeding into the physical stages, the system engineers and managers involved, will seek approval from the appropriate groups of people. Within the physical stages and during the construction of the system, the system builders will test and make the necessary alterations to the modules being implemented.

The users' systems acceptance will include all the necessary documentation and all the training and support required to ensure that the new system or module is successful.

DATA PROCESSING

In the past, the majority of data processing has been carried out by companies using batch style computer systems. With the cost of hardware rapidly reducing and with the hardware power and facilities increasing inversely, on-line systems are now becoming easier to justify and develop.

The objectives of data processing are to capture data, process it and present the information. Because of the widespread use of computers within business, it is sometimes assumed that data always refers to some type of financially oriented transaction.

In fact, data has a more general meaning. In general terms, data can be used to denote any or all facts, numbers, letters and symbols that refer to, or describe an object, idea, condition, or any other function. But data can only be of value if it can be organised in some way, so that it becomes meaningful to somebody - this is information.

The data must be checked for integrity, to ensure that errors have not arisen during any data capture processes. Data are compared to establish relationships, similarities and differences. By now the data should have been completely processed, but to be proper information the processing results must be presented in such a way that it has relevance and meaning. Finally, the information must be produced on a medium that is legible.

INFORMATION TECHNOLOGY

Of all the major problems encountered in computing, the most difficult is the management of the systems and their development. Unlike any engineering or architectural drawings, the systems cannot be visibly represented as a model. Any building or machine can be shown as a set of drawings and as a three dimensional model, but the design and the build of the system cannot be seen, nor can it be represented on top of a desk.

In the case of an architectural concept, the designer will draw the plans and will supervise and delegate the tasks to builders to construct in a fashion, as close to perfect logistics as possible.

In modern Information Technology and computing in general, structured methodologies are used, where dataflow diagrams can be drawn, data can be modelled and at the end of the logical phase, the system can be prototyped and programmed.

This brings forward the problem of managing, delegating, and guiding those who analyse the business requirements and the data on which the information is based, the professionals who proceed with the design based on the requirements and those who program and implement the required system.

In most cases, these activities are under one roof. Mainly, three different professions passing details to each other at the end of each developmental stage; Analysis, Designing and Programming. The Information Technology Manager will need to know what each step of development involves and at every phase what the professional system engineer is doing. As in every other project, tasks need to be based on timescales and the financial implication to remain close to the budgets.

In commercial computing the financial costs for developing a new system are in six figures and in many cases where additional hardware and software are to be acquired, one project can be in the region of millions of pounds. To cope with such enormities of resources and the correct availability of business information, an organisation relies completely on the professional knowledge of its system engineers and those who manage the projects.

The media frequently report failures of systems and frustrations in computers at large. More often within companies, disappointments in systems are such that the computer department is totally isolated from other business activities. Yet, there are those companies whose total running of their business is based on the smooth running of their computer systems; the profitability and the revenue always ahead of their competitors.

But, it is also true to say that with all modern computing and devices, industry still suffers, or outputs could be improved, if only the computer department could design and operate a system the way the users work and based on the company's requirements.

The systems person is aware of these problems and yet cannot stretch his/her know-how any more than is already done. Imagine the various professionals under one roof, the complexity of designing and constructing systems, of the housekeeping involved, of the running and maintenance of all these sections.

If an organisation has many departments to enable it to function, so does the computer environment. In a superimposed mode, the Information Technology Manager has just as many sections to look after, admittedly on a smaller scale, but just as complex. Humans, machines, finances, stresses, productions, outputs, man-machine relationships, all in one department, just as much as any overall organisation is facing.

The I.T. Manager relies on management skills, systems knowledge and various other business methods in order to give a good service to everybody in the company. The subject covers business computing and its management, the development of new systems, the implementation and their running. The Manager in computing is aware of actual examples and will draw on projects and experience gained in building large and moderate systems based on what the users require, their problems, the solutions and their training in ensuring the success of the new system, or additional information technology modules.

In the first place, the expertise of those involved must cover the last generation of computing (which systems are still operating in many international organisations), its successes and its failures and the running in company environments. This includes the mainframe-based systems, the advent of PCs (Personal Computers) and their impact on networking and distributed processing, expert systems, shells and artificial intelligence.

These, inevitably will be supported by training and experience in Structured Methodologies, a comparative study into methods, the use of the predominant systems architectures and a method for 'Rapid Building' system engineering.

Modern systems engineering, concentrates on the training aspect, the psychology of users, motivation and delegating specific to the computer departments, the interviewing techniques in gathering the information on current systems, the cataloguing of the problems and requirements, the appropriate solutions and their incorporation into the design of the required system.

Regarding the newcomers to the commercial computing professions, organisations rely on aspiring young graduates. With all good will they bring with them and with all their ambitions for the yuppie incomes, graduates still need the specialised training in computing and systems applications to business requirements.

It must be said that academia has progressed enormously in computing during the last ten years, but business needs differ from that of university research and studies. Graduates who enter the companies' surroundings find that they are unprepared for the demand of creating and using commercial systems in large organisations.

SYSTEMS ARCHITECTURE

The background of structured analysis and designing as an information engineering methodology, a technique-driven approach, started in 1972. Between 1980 and 1982, Gane and Sarson and Yourdon methodologies were extensively used. In 1983, business started using the information engineering automated version. By 1989, the information engineering development paths underwent further evolution. In 1992, the business re-engineering and object-oriented versions were introduced.

The need to control and manage the ever-increasing amounts of all organisational data being created, particularly computer-generated data, has gained recognition. However, because data management automates the processes used within a company, implementation is not easy. Several data management suppliers have begun requesting that a full systems and business analysis is undertaken prior to system implementation.

These show not only where existing processes need to be changed but determines exactly what the data management system needs to do within each unique organisation. It, therefore, provides the platform for successful systems architecture and management introduction and avoids the many pitfalls that so many companies have experienced in attempting to develop and install a new management system.

Rapid prototyping is gaining acceptance. Companies are using this method to obtain system design models in weeks rather than months, dramatically reducing lead-times and enabling better decisions and choice of system modules to be made.

A Systems Engineer in his/her approach defines the whole project, modularises it into manageable sections and proceeds in a logical manner according to the clear principles of user involvement.

The tasks are always broken down into structured goal-oriented, meaningful units of work. The end result of these structured sets of tasks is applicable to the development path of analysis, design and construction.

New techniques have been introduced that dramatically reduce the time taken to solve business and system problems. The result is that it is now possible to take the requirements, analyse and view the results in days or weeks, rather than months. This, of course, makes analysis possible and cost-effective within the design process, rather than a special system task.

Recent years have seen further development in business and systems analysis software. Product releases of leading software houses have not only made systems architecture easier for everyday system engineers, but faster too. Closer links to CASE (Computer-aided Software Engineering) systems have made analysis simpler, while new interfaces make analysis understandable to users.

DESIGNING SYSTEMS

The interface between the user and a computer system has always been an important design factor. In interactive computer systems the interface (the dialogue) can influence not only the system's efficiency, but also its acceptability to the user.

The user psychology here is extremely important. The interface between the user and the system must be an extension of the way the user does his/her work. Any dialogue which causes deviation from this, will cause frustration and ultimately dislike for the system.

The new technology is introducing techniques which are changing the way organisations work, as opposed to just addressing existing tasks. To successfully implement and apply the systems tools requires extensive education and it is this that is currently presenting the biggest hurdles for companies.

SECURITY AND SYSTEM ASSURANCE

Computer security has become a challenge dominated by the improvements to the technology of computers. Techniques are being developed to make access to systems harder. In recent years, much work has been done to make the computer recognise individual characteristics, unique to the user, such as a signature, a fingerprint, or even the genetic print of DNA.

With users and companies becoming more dependent upon computer systems, the privacy and reliability of such systems are becoming critical aspects of design. Systems Assurance, a term which is currently popular, of a system embraces the parts of systems design which reduce the risk of both the fraudulent use of the system and lengthy recovery times in the event of a system's failure.

Users and companies are becoming more and more dependent upon resilience of computer-based systems.

In various sensitive applications, frequent auditing is recommended. As a minimum, a daily control report should be produced, reconciling balances on the opening and closing versions of data sets. This report should, also, show in detail the origins of all transactions processed during the reporting period.

With the number of computer applications continuing to grow and with a similar increase in the number of people using them, a new type of back-up service is needed. To meet the demand, a number of companies have introduced guides to their applications, which include catalogues on CD ROM. The catalogue, in fact, serves as a comprehensive system engineering tool.

Details on system applications, specifications and service requirements are made available to all users. If a user is not sure what documents are needed, he/she can start by looking at the full index.

Companies are even making available dedicated internal e-mail messages and Internet pages. Newsletters are published, which keep the users informed of new product developments, interesting applications and other IT activities.

The widespread use of computers throughout business and the rapid growth of Internet connectivity mean that computer security should concern all organisations.

However, it involves more topics than might be supposed. Ranging from the technicalities of protecting networks, tele-working and mobile systems, through the legalities of computer crime and corporate responsibility, to the politics of registering and protecting encryption keys.

Extremely sophisticated identification systems now exist that can read retina patterns, fingerprints and infra-red emissions from faces.

One simple measure to prevent unauthorised outsiders dialling into the system is to install dial-back modems. However, this security measure is easy to side-step. Likewise, calling-line identification, which permits the computer to identify the calling number and refuse access if it not recognised, can be bypassed by the experienced people.

Encryption is essential for the transmission of any material passing down the line. A simple method is to employ software which uses the same code at either end to encode and decode data. The next level is to impose a code of the day, using an encryption device card which is synchronised with a similar calculator card within the network.

SOFTWARE CONSIDERATIONS

Developing large systems require a range of software to achieve the overall systems objective. Depending upon the application and hardware types, this range of software at best could be totally packaged, or at worst may need to be completely written specially for the system.

Software in a project is like a jigsaw puzzle. Each piece fulfils a role and each piece must integrate with other pieces to make the complete system.

Applying hardware and software knowledge to system engineering and the development of systems enables System Architects to choose individual applications from a range of developers and bring these together into a single system that best meets the needs of the company and its tasks, transparently, sharing data. It also enables standard software, such as spreadsheets, word-processing, presentation packages and databases, to be linked to engineering software.

The flexibility this gives is far better for users than the traditional closed systems environment that forms the basis of many engineering software packages. However, to take advantage of this environment the system developers must totally restructure their approach to system building, a complex and daunting task.

SYSTEMS MANAGEMENT

The majority of organisations recognise that the effective use of information is vital to their success. Successful companies build enormous knowledge bases that reside in their corporate files, their information centres and in the brains of their busy executives. This knowledge and experience is the organisation's power base and their competitive edge.

To remain competitive they must be able to find information at the right time, in the right place and in the format that is easy to use.

When the IT department manages the information derived from the systems, effectively, the company in turn gains real value from information. The IT department and its management of information must maintain a leading position in the specialised world of commercial computing.

The IT department will certainly benefit by having a network of specialists providing knowledge, experience and technical skills to suit most types of company demands.

Instant access to corporate information means better decisions, reduced costs and increased profits. To facilitate such a service, the IT department must work with a wide range of other departments and their staff. Many of the users are looking for help, or advice from the information management area.

This means that the IT staff must be prepared to undertake all sizes of projects, their development and the management of such systems. This entails a project management system which, together with the chosen methodology, will ensure the success of the information services.

STRUCTURED MANAGEMENT METHODS

Many users believe that a project must involve computers in some way. However, a much broader view is required when one considers that a project is set up to deliver a business product. In other words, a projects temporary, which only exists to deliver something considered worthwhile to the business.

The resulting product may be for any application (manual or otherwise, clerical, management style, production of goods, engineering in general), including a computer system. In this case, the environment created and the work done to deliver the product is a project.

In some cases, projects may not deliver what was expected and costly investment produces few benefits. It is little wonder that things go wrong and projects fail, not because people are ineffective, but because of the sheer complexity of project management.

Over the years it has become recognised that there is a common thread running through the management of projects. Much of this is common sense and it is the formulation of this rational thinking and management good practice, into a structure, which gives rise to project methods.

There are many project management methods available, each of which is characterised by the way in which it provides principles, procedures and techniques for the management of projects. Methods utilise existing standard techniques as well as introducing their own unique features.

The number of project failures can be dramatically reduced by the proper application of a structured project management method; a method which provides project management principles and processes to address the problems.

A number of project management methods provide a variety of approaches. Traditional project management and other management methods plan and control against a list of activities. Some specially designed for the information systems project environment. Such procedures are applied to many types and sizes of project. This, therefore, gives the advantage of common standards being applied to the management of systems projects.

Using a management method will ensure that a system is built for the users and for the benefit of the business. Quality is of paramount importance to all IT departments. There are a few official national and international standards in information management, so an important feature of the structured management method approach is to create a de facto environment where standards can interrelate as they evolve.

A structured management method provides management with the ability to react swiftly and efficiently to business and strategy changes, to understand what projects and studies are in hand and their interrelationships both, with each other and with the overall strategy. It, also, provides an effective way of controlling costs and resources at the business level.

All management methods demand the participation of senior management in any type of project; from the initial stage to the phase where a completed system is handed over to the user community. A project, also, needs the involvement of quality assurance and other support staff, where all the participants form the steering committee and the support groups.

The committee and all participating follow a project management method, comprising integrated procedures, based on a number of principles and documented in a set of procedural manuals.

The overall objective of the structured management method is to enable the right people to make the right decision at the right time. This formally enforces the involvement and commitment of the business, users and technical interest in a project.

Plans are the basis of the management of any project. They provide the benchmark of information required for decision making, controlling, communicating and reporting.

The objectives of each meeting are defined and guidance is provided on the agenda and procedures. In certain projects, it is recognised that there may be a requirement to control the work of the project in more detail.

Project management methods are concentrating on the things to be produced, rather than the activities required producing them. These things are called products and the approach ensures that all products are identified and clearly defined before proceeding with activity planning. It is a significant aid to better estimating and planning.

A structured management method, also, provides detailed guidance on the procedures and techniques required to apply the principles.

The application of the procedures and techniques is flexible and it is this aspect which makes a management method practical and successful.

MANAGEMENT OF PROJECTS

A project management system should be utilised on all sizeable projects undertaken. A Project Manager should be appointed, responsible for the agreement and delivery of project products to agreed deadlines throughout the project's lifecycle. The Project Manager should produce a weekly status report which will be provided one day prior to a weekly progress meeting.

During the project lifecycle, project issues can occur which require analysis, documentation and resolutions. Any change to the requirements, or to any document once it has been formally agreed, is subject to the following change control procedures. Throughout the life of the project, reviews of critical documents are necessary.

The strategy of the system acceptance will be defined by the user. The subsequent plan and test scripts will be based upon the standards. As part of a quality management system, a senior manager undertakes the auditing of the project. The quality auditor operates outside the design and builds team structures.

Before delivery of the system, a training schedule for the users will be agreed. Additionally, prior to any handing over, the system will be tested and should any problems arise, these will be reported and remedied before the users sign off.

RECRUITING IN COMPUTING

With the state-of-the-art in commercial computing, the accelerated progress in technology and the demand made on more systems development, the IT management find themselves increasingly occupied in the selection of larger number of specialised staff. Such is the great weight on IT managers, to fulfil new job responsibilities and to replace those who leave for greener pastures.

The vacancies for system engineers are constantly increasing, at such a rate that a new industry has developed. Additional to the traditional recruitment, the demand for the supply of contractors, mainly for systems analysis and programming, has increased in proportions. Agencies for freelancers are now deeply rooted as a service to IT.

The contracting analysts/programmers are in their thousands and agencies in their hundreds. The cost to the organisation for such a service is huge, often enough remuneration paid being higher than what the business directors are paid. Frequently more than the IT manager gets. With such numbers of candidates involved and an unknown expertise at that, the systems managers are faced with the additional responsibility of frequent interviews and uncertainty as to what kind of know-how they will obtain from contractors.

The agencies do not have the knowledge to scrutinise every system engineer on their registers. It is a well known fact that the agents submit the CVs of individuals without even checking on the contractor's experience. The agencies arrange for the interviews between the company's managers and the freelancers over the telephone. For this kind of service the agencies receive between 20% and 40% of the contracting fees. The larger, established contracting agencies have a firm charge of 33% commission.

The IT management and their staff are faced with the overload of interviews. It is an under-estimated task. With all the pressures from within the systems areas, it is a wonder how systems can be developed and become operational within the quoted timescales and costs.

As an example - using the two extremes of the systems engineering professions of Analysts and Programmers. It is of paramount importance to use the right techniques for interviewing systems staff. In hiring systems engineers, it must be remembered that an analyst is the person who keeps in touch with the users and the programmer is the one that builds the system.

The analyst must be an out-going person, a good mixer - a person who can get on with other people, easily collect information and details and must be a good systems representative - the psychological personality type of an extrovert thinker.

On the other extreme, bear in mind that the programmer has to decipher the documents the analyst produces, in order to start constructing the required system. This makes the programmer the psychological personality of an introvert sensation type.

There are many other types of professionals within systems engineering: Designers, database administrators, operators, strategists, and a few more. In interviewing, therefore, the interviewer will be helped enormously if he/she makes a few notes beforehand regarding the type of person needed to fill in the responsibilities within the systems professions.

In interviewing, handing out a short narrative and asking the interviewee to turn it into diagrams and programming coding is not on. The candidate must be relaxed, made to feel wanted, important and then prompted to expand on items relevant to the vacancy.

Systems engineering is such a modern profession, its responsibilities and qualities are hardly known to psychologists, psychometrists and professional recruiters. For instance, one cannot rely on aptitude testing alone, as there are no set rules. Experience in systems areas and knowing what is needed is the best guide and basis for the interview.

Within the various scales of recruitment are the newcomers to the professions of systems management; the graduates of IT 'hybrid' management and the MBAs, whose degree material is based on traditional management. Commercial computing demands organisational experience gained within business functions relating to systems.

The young graduates of the first degree education can be recruited with the proviso that they get trained within the business parameters. It is true that the new universities in their computing sciences subjects cover methodologies, databases and programming, but the question still prevails, as to which extend of commercial experience is embedded in the lecturers and their tutorials and those running the academic departments. Let it be stressed that this statement refers to the business computing and systems development in the commercial world.

Universities have progressed enormously in their research on artificial intelligence and other fields such as parallelism. The outside world still runs systems on mainframes and applications as required by the users. The modern construction of business systems and tools developed, suit the personalities and the abilities of those who use these applications.

Faced with such problems, the IT management pays a lot of attention to interviewing. After all, like any other recruitment, employing a human being (permanent or contractor) is still a big investment of time, costs and other resources.

It must be added, that the interviewing techniques in commercial computing are applied to applicants for vacant positions, as well as the users who ask for new systems, the repairing of an existing one, or the extraction of the data based information.

Interviewing is the most commonly used way of acquiring basic concepts and requirements from the users. It is an activity that needs careful planning and execution. It is crucial to plan an interview to ensure that it is as productive as possible.

As an interviewer, practise the art of relaxation on you and then apply the technique to the candidate. Remember that the users interviewed may offer details on what they think you want to know. A good analyst will steer the discussion to the domain of interest, whereas a job applicant will be nervous, anxious and feel as if on the receiving end.

PROJECT CONTROL IN SYSTEMS

Businesses have problems which they need to solve. They, also, have requirements which altogether enable the smooth running of their environment. To establish the appropriate running of the business organisation, projects need to be set.

An organisation is probably undergoing significant change. Changes span functional boundaries, case conflict and concern and present a major risk to the business and those managers responsible for the development of systems. Many companies are now adopting a project-based approach to managing the change of systems and their development.

Managers of today and of the future, require skills in managing projects. These skills are supplementary to the line management skills. A company needs to enhance business planning and control structures to explicitly link system implementation to business led projects and programmes.

A project in information technology is a temporary situation within the working groups (the system users) and the computing management, with the objective of delivering a product. The resulting product relies on the project progress and how it is approached in its scope to deliver.

Unlike existing systems operational management, where one deals with established computer services, project management encounters the unfamiliar, new problems and needs for change.

In managing a project, a list of activities will not be enough. The project must be product-based. A methodology needs to be followed, procedures to be applied.

The appropriate procedures, therefore, give the advantage of common standards being applied to the management of all projects, with directional emphasis to meeting the corporate objectives.

Project management supports the implementation of the business strategies with explicit link to the development plan. This provides management with the ability to react swiftly and efficiently to any changes, to understand the project stages and steps in hand and their relationship with each other. It, also, provides an effective way of controlling costs and resources at all levels.

The appropriate analysis and design methodology will assist the project team members to concentrate on the system components to be produced. It enables the management and the analysts to identify and clearly define all the development phases. It is, also, a significant contributor to quality, better estimating and planning.

SYSTEMS DEVELOPMENT PROCEDURES

The system specification procedures form the basis within the conventional business environment for setting out the standards for system development. They describe a step by step approach to developing and implementing computer systems. They define the documents to be produced, the controls to be applied and the tasks to be performed.

The intention is that these procedures be applied flexibly. On the other hand, the phases are designed for sequential development, with the output from one phase being the input to the next, all leading to the eventual implementation of the system. Project plans should be drawn up to suit the particular project and then adhered to.

The procedures define the paths that will be followed in projects set up to develop computer systems. A project is, thus, described in terms of its major divisions (Phases), its Control Points, the Activities that are accomplished in each phase and the Tasks that go to make up those activities.

A project starts with an initiation and ends with a review and user training. The Project Initiation Document (PID) will incite the feasibility study and the terms of reference. The review will include the report to the users and the appropriate steps for the system training and the training manual distributed to all the users involved in the running of the system-to-be.

The system development lifecycle, in outlining the activities to be followed and the tasks to be carried out in a project, provides the framework for planning and defining a project.

The development lifecycle does not ensure that projects will meet a particular level of quality, nor does it ensure that work carried out will be both, efficient and effective. That is a matter of how people perform and it is the goal of project management to make sure that conditions exist for them to be efficient and effective.

The framework of the lifecycle with its different phases, offers some guidance on when project management should be applied. Each phase has a beginning, middle and end. Project management procedures are ongoing and required to fit in with the dimensions of the workday and reporting cycles.

The performance of any computer department can only be judged by the service given to the system users. This clearly means business change through projects. It involves people and the experience they carry with them. Experience in system building when a company needs it most; when this type of people, the best in the organisation is in short supply and great demand. They are usually, therefore, not available when needed for a critical new project - to develop the long awaited system.

SYSTEMS SPECIFICATION

The System Specification starts as far back as Systems Analysis and is not completed until programming begins. A standard is required for conducting systems design because a uniform approach is needed across all projects to ensure understanding and consistency.

The standard outputs are required as input to programming activities. The systems specifications, therefore, need to be written in a rigorous and consistent manner to ensure that all user requirements are catered for and all business processing is completely and accurately defined and documented.

The System Specification is the phase where the lowest level dataflow diagrams and descriptions from process analysis are pulled together.

PROCESS ANALYSIS

The aim is to reach a detailed logical design sufficient for all specification work. A standard is required for conducting process analysis because a uniform approach is needed across all projects. It concentrates on processes rather than data. Thorough process analysis encourages understanding of the system and user environment. The outputs from the process analysis are required for the system design processes.

There can be many inputs into process analysis depending on the nature and complexity of the project.

The dataflow diagram is a powerful input to design because it identifies the data flows, data stores and processing involved. The technique is top-down; an overview followed by increasingly lower levels of detail.

SYSTEM REVIEWS

The purpose of a review is to define the process for understanding what is needed and as means of checking the quality of work throughout the systems development lifecycle.

It is clear that in practice it would not be appropriate to subject all outputs to the same level of review and several variants of the review process are required.

PHYSICAL DESIGN

Physical design converts the results of process and data design into an implementable computer solution and defines the computer/clerical interface. This is evaluated against the requirements and amended as appropriate.

The scope of the physical design is to cover the technical design of application systems. It concentrates on the design of the system processes, rather than the design of databases.

Requirements often change during the design phase and new ones emerge. In addition, it often raises more questions requiring further analysis. Therefore, the final design may only be arrived at through several iterations of logical and physical design.

ECONOMIC AFFAIRS

Americans would likely remember 1999 as the most prosperous year in at least three decades. Even so, businesspeople, investors, and workers wondered whether the boom was a miracle of technology-generated productivity or a speculative bubble.

Most of the spectacular performance of the stock indexes was accounted for by a relatively small number of companies. These included semiconductor producers such as Intel, computer manufacturers such as Dell, "solutions" companies such as IBM, and, most dramatically, the Internet companies, or "dot.coms," such as Amazon.com (Jeff Bezos), America Online (AOL), Yahoo, and Priceline.com. Outside this favoured circle, many profitable companies that did not have dramatic "new economy" stories saw their stock prices drift lower.

Many American businesspeople had developed a mild pity or even contempt for their European counterparts over the course of the 1990s. There was a collective belief that the political structure of Europe, with the exception of the U.K., would effectively keep the continent from catching up with U.S. productivity and growth. There were exceptional European enterprises, of course, such as Airbus Industrie, and SAP AG, the German developer of "enterprise management" software.

The euro, the new unified European Union (EU) currency, was launched in January 1999. Much promoted by EU officials as an alternative to the dollar as an international currency and store of value, it embarrassed its sponsors by dropping some 14% in value against the U.S. dollar over the course of 1999.

While the financial underpinnings of the U.S. economy were somewhat shaky, however, the country had spent a huge amount on computers and software and on telecommunications networks tying all those machines together. The most dramatic beneficiary of this was the telecommunications industry, which had to meet a seemingly insatiable demand for "bandwidth," or message-carrying capacity. The biggest single impetus for this demand was the expansion of Internet traffic. Transmissions via the Internet included more complex graphics, sound, and full-motion visual images, all of which required either high-capacity cable or fibre-optic cable that had the necessary bandwidth. In 1999, fibre-optic cable capacity was being increased by 100% every nine months. Cellular telephones and wireless data transmission also continued to expand; 31% of American consumers had cellular phones by the end of 1999, up from 25% just two years earlier.

As late as the 1980s, the telecommunications industry had been financially stable and was growing at a moderate pace. By 1999 there were winning companies such as Qualcomm, Inc., which developed an innovative, high-quality cellular-telephone technology. Its stock rose more than 20-fold in the year, and it had revenues of nearly $4 billion. By way of contrast, Iridium, Inc. a "go-anywhere" mobile phone company that depended on a multibillion-dollar array of satellites, went bankrupt in July, its equity effectively wiped out and its bonds dropping to 17 cents on the dollar. An industry that had been composed of steady monopolies turned into a competitive free-for-all.

The demand for new and replacement personal computers also held up in 1999, propelled partly by price cuts, partly by the appeal of fast new machines, and partly by a perceived need to get "Y2K (Year 2000) compliant" systems in place before the year 2000. The computer software industry underwent two revolutionary shocks. First was the successful antitrust suit by the U.S. Department of Justice against Microsoft Corp., which was seen as a potential cause for a break up of the company. Ironically, however, any harsh treatment of the company would have to face the political reality that a large fraction of the middle-class public owned Microsoft shares, and that could easily lead to a backlash against the government litigation. The judge's finding against

Microsoft also led to an increasing investor and user interest in computer operating systems other than Microsoft's own Windows system. The major beneficiaries were companies that wrote software based on the open Linux operating system.

The second shock for the software industry was the extent to which companies writing large "enterprise software" programs were losing market share to companies that based their applications on Internet protocols. This could be seen as part of the "democratization" or "networking" of software. The enterprise software companies such as the German SAP, or PeopleSoft Inc. and Oracle Corp. in the United States, had based their communications within corporate communications networks on proprietary software rather than the increasingly popular Internet. SAP, which made its name by offering one large system to tie together all the elements of a company's computing, saw its reputation hurt by the difficulties several large companies such as Hershey Foods Corp. had in implementing the huge, monolithic programs.

Perhaps the most remarkable phenomenon in the valuation of companies was the extraordinary stock market performance of the "pure" Internet companies. These companies, few of which earned any profits during the year, saw increases in their stock prices of up to several thousand percent. These valuations could not be based on increases in profits or even revenues but were based just on investors' hopes that at some distant point in the future a selection of companies using the Internet would be able to displace established commercial competitors using "bricks and mortar" facilities. Despite the high stock prices of companies such as Amazon.com or Priceline.com, there was an increasing realization that moving commerce to the Internet would still require conventional facilities. This led to enormous interest in the public stock offering of United Parcel Service, whose trucks were needed to deliver many of the items ordered on-line from the Internet companies.

Growth in high-tech companies had a spill-over effect on other American industries.

INDUSTRY DEVELOPMENTS

By the first quarter of 1997, Apple's share of the U.S. personal computer (PC) market had fallen sharply to 3.3% as customers continued to favour PCs that ran Microsoft Corp.'s Windows operating system (OS). It was a troubled year for Apple Computer Inc. already weakened by declining computer sales, Apple was in turmoil in July when Chairman and CEO Gilbert F. Amelio resigned from the company after some 18 months on the job, during which Apple lost nearly $1.5 billion. Apple's board of directors reportedly was displeased by falling sales of Apple's Macintosh computers. Though Amelio, who had been welcomed as a corporate turnaround specialist, was unsuccessful, the roots of Apple's troubles ran deep. They were said to include lack of technical innovation, product-handling mistakes, and management upheaval, plus thousands of layoffs.

The year also marked the return of Apple cofounder Steve Jobs, an articulate but temperamental leader who had been pressured to resign as chairman in 1985. Beginning as an unpaid Amelio adviser in December 1996 after his firm, NeXT Software, Inc., was acquired by Apple for more than $400 million, Jobs stepped up his participation in Apple's management as the company tried to find a way back from the brink. In August he announced that Microsoft, a long time rival of Apple, would buy $150 million in nonvoting Apple stock. Although the Mac OS competed with Windows, it was believed that Microsoft, which sold a substantial amount of applications software to the Macintosh market, had much to gain by helping its competitor remain in business. In September Jobs became interim CEO. During the same month, most of the Apple board of directors resigned, and Apple agreed to buy Power Computing Corp., a Macintosh clone manufacturer, for $100 million, in effect halting the corporate strategy of allowing others to produce clone copies of the Macintosh under license.

Microsoft had no financial problems but ran into difficulty with the federal government. In October it was accused by the U.S. Justice Department of violating the 1995 court order barring it from anticompetitive licensing activities. The Justice Department asked a federal court to impose a $1 million-a-day fine on the software industry leader for requiring PC manufacturers to use Microsoft's World Wide Web browser, Internet Explorer, on their machines when they installed Microsoft's Windows 95 OS. As evidence, the Justice Department said Compaq Computer Corp. claimed that it was threatened with the loss of its license to use Windows 95 if it removed Internet Explorer from some of its PCs. Microsoft said antitrust regulators were mistaken and that it would defend its position; it called the disagreement with Compaq an ordinary dispute over licensing terms.

The Microsoft-Justice Department battle had the potential to have a major impact on the marketing contest between Microsoft and Netscape Communications Corp., both of which were trying to make their own browser the most widely used on the Internet. Justice Department attorneys said they were trying to prevent Microsoft, which had a virtual monopoly in personal computer operating systems, from using that power to take control of the Internet browser market. At issue was the Justice Department's interpretation of a 1995 consent decree with Microsoft that had settled another antitrust dispute. Microsoft said that far from violating the agreement, it was merely making technological improvements to its existing Windows 95 product by adding browser software to it.

Another industry leader, Intel Corp. under Chairman and CEO Andrew Grove, also drew the interest of federal government regulators. Intel, the world's leading manufacturer of microprocessor chips for PCs, learned in September that it was being investigated by the Federal Trade Commission (FTC) in connection with its business practices in the PC market. The FTC said it wanted to determine if Intel had tried to monopolize or otherwise restrict price competition in its role as supplier of about 85% of the microprocessors used in PCs. Intel also was the subject of an antitrust investigation by the FTC from 1991 to 1993 that did not result in any action against the company.

In a surprising move, Digital Equipment Corp. sued Intel in May, alleging that Intel's Pentium microprocessor chips violated as many as 10 Digital patents. Intel denied that it used Digital technology in the Pentium chip, but the suit, which sought unspecified damages, had the potential to cost Intel billions of dollars as well as cripple its ability to use the Pentium technology. The suit also had the potential to disrupt the entire PC industry by forcing Intel to redesign its Pentium chips.

The dispute involved Digital's Alpha microprocessor. Digital claimed that Intel had access to proprietary information about the chip in 1990, when it was evaluating whether to license the Alpha technology from Digital. Intel responded by suing Digital for the return of information about Intel's next-generation Pentium chips. Since many Digital computers depended on Intel chips, Intel's apparent intent was to hurt Digital's computer-development efforts and put Digital at a competitive disadvantage in the PC market. In August Intel filed a counterclaim that alleged Digital had violated 14 Intel patents. Intel claimed that the technologies the patents represented were widely used throughout Digital's product line.

In the end the legal storm passed almost as fast as it began. In October Intel said it would buy Digital's Alpha chip development and manufacturing operations for $700 million as part of an agreement to end their legal wrangling. Digital would keep its Alpha design teams to work on future versions of the chip. The deal also included a series of patent cross-licensing agreements for which Intel would pay Digital an undisclosed sum. Both companies said their lawsuits against each other would be kept on hold, pending government approval of the agreement.

A battle over software standards also escalated into a major lawsuit. Sun Microsystems sued Microsoft in October in a battle for control of Java language software standards. Sun's suit claimed that Microsoft's Internet Explorer 4.0 software contained a variant of Sun's Java programming language that differed from the standard version. Sun accused Microsoft of infringing on Sun's Java trademark, false advertising, and breach of contract, unfair competition, and interference. Microsoft denied Sun's allegations and countersued, seeking a dismissal of the Sun suit and asking the court to uphold Microsoft's right to claim that its products were "Java compatible."

There were indications of at least one impending class-action lawsuit against several computer makers for allegedly continuing to sell PCs that could not cope with the "year 2000 problem." This problem, also called the "Millennium Bug," had arisen because old computer systems designed to use a two-digit date to represent the year (e.g., 97 to represent 1997) could fail on Jan. 1, 2000, when faced with the two-digit date 00; they would read this as 1900.

Consolidation continued in the fast-changing computing market. In February 3Com Corp. made the surprise announcement that it would merge with U.S. Robotics Corp., a leading manufacturer of high-speed modems, in a $6.6 billion exchange of stock. The intent was to build one of the largest companies in the rapidly growing field of computer networking. Japanese computer maker NEC Corp. announced in December that it was increasing its stake in Packard Bell NEC, Inc., from 20% to 49%.

In April Microsoft acquired WebTV Networks, which sold units that allowed people to connect to the Internet directly through their television sets, for $425 million. The software company said it wanted to "dramatically accelerate the merger of the Internet and television." In a similar move, Sun Microsystems in July said it would acquire Diba, a maker of Internet set-top boxes that could compete with Microsoft, but terms of that deal were not disclosed. As part of Sun, Diba was to work with consumer electronics companies to provide Internet-ready TVs, set-top boxes, satellite reception boxes, and "smart" telephones.

Compaq's purchase of Tandem Computers for $4 billion in stock was completed in August. Compaq was a major manufacturer of PCs and PC server computers and Tandem pioneered highly reliable machines called fault-tolerant computer systems. In September America Online Inc. (AOL) agreed to buy its biggest competitor, the CompuServe Inc. on-line service. While CompuServe would continue as a separate operation, it would be operated by AOL, which would then have a combined customer list of more than 11 million subscribers. In a complex deal a third company, telecommunications firm WorldCom, was to buy CompuServe from H&R Block for $1.2 billion in stock and then exchange CompuServe's Interactive Services division for $175 million and AOL's ANS Communications. In the end, WorldCom was to become AOL's largest network service provider.

INTERNET RETAILING

In 1998 consumers could purchase virtually anything over the Internet. Books, compact discs, computers, stocks, and even new and used automobiles were widely available from World Wide Web sites that seemed to spring up almost daily. A few years earlier, sceptics had predicted that consumers accustomed to shopping in stores would be reluctant to buy items that they could not see or touch in person. For a growing number of time-starved consumers, however, shopping from their home computer was proving to be a convenient, cost-effective alternative to driving to the store.

For all the consumer interest, retailing in cyberspace was still a largely unprofitable business, however. Internet pioneer Amazon.com, which began selling books in 1995 and later branched into recorded music and videos, posted revenue of $153.7 million in the third quarter, up from $37.9 million in the same period of 1997. Overall, however, the company's loss widened to $45.2 million from $9.6 million, and analysts did not expect the company to turn a profit until 2001. Despite gushing red ink, Amazon.com had a stock market value of many billions, reflecting investors' unbridled optimism about the future of the industry.

Internet retailing appealed to investors because it provided an efficient means for reaching millions of consumers without incurring the cost of operating brick-and-mortar stores with their armies of salespeople.

Mergers and acquisitions were also common as competitors girded for the future. CDnow Inc. and N2K Inc., two of the largest on-line music retailers, agreed to merge, creating a formidable opponent to Amazon.com's compact disc business. Meanwhile, German media giant Bertelsmann AG agreed to buy 50% of Barnes & Noble Inc.'s on-line book business, providing yet another threat to Amazon.com.

DEVELOPMENTS IN JAPAN

The year 1992 was a difficult one for computer manufacturers and software houses in Japan because of a combination of saturated international markets and the prolonged recession. The production of computers and related equipment in 1992 (January-December) amounted to 5,616,700,000,000 yen, a 7.7% decrease from 6,083,400,000,000 yen in 1991.

Investment in information equipment declined especially sharply in the financial and security industries, but this belt-tightening mood also spread to manufacturing. Most vendors predicted little or no recovery in 1993. According to the statistics based on the Ministry of International Trade and Industry's New Survey on Computers Deliveries, the total number of deliveries of computers in 1992 was 2,712,505, and the value of the deliveries was 3,794,300,000 yen. Both the numbers and the value of the deliveries decreased from the preceding year.

Included in this survey were all types of hardware - general-purpose computers, minicomputers, office computers and distributed processing processors, workstations, and PCs. In terms of the value of the deliveries, general-purpose computers ranked first with a 48.1% share, followed by personal computers (24.7%), and office computers/distributed processing processors (13.8%).

According to a survey by JEIDA (Japan Electronic Industry Development Association), the shipment of personal computers in fiscal 1991 totalled 2,310,000 in terms of central processing units, down 13.2% from the preceding year. They totalled 1,172,900,000,000 yen in monetary value, down 7.1%. Influenced by the worsening economic environment, shipments decreased from the previous year for the first time since the survey began in fiscal 1981.

COMPUTERS AND INFORMATION SYSTEMS

Two forces dominated developments in the computer industry in 1995 - the arrival of Microsoft Corp.'s new Windows 95 personal computer (PC) operating system and the overnight ascendancy of the Internet and the World Wide Web, a subset of the Internet designed for multimedia use.

Events in 1995 drew so much attention to both Windows and the Web that by year's end the computer mouse had become almost as well known to the world's population at large as the television set remote control. In fact, the trends that played out during 1995 led many to argue that a computer mouse might soon be used as much as the TV remote control to call up everything from computer-served movies on demand to news stories and E-mail from friends and families. The decline of the well-known supercomputer company Cray Computer Corp., which filed for bankruptcy in March, was further evidence of the growing dominance of the PC industry.

Windows 95, which made its world debut on August 24 accompanied by a $300 million global advertising campaign, was a major overhaul of Microsoft's Windows operating environment, which added a "point-and-click" operating system known as a graphic user interface, or GUI, to the text-based disk operating system, or DOS, used in most PCs.

The graphic World Wide Web evolved in academic computer laboratories during the early 1990s as software originally developed by the European particle physics consortium CERN, headquartered in Geneva, was adapted to allow people using the global Internet computer network to use the same sort of graphic manipulations available in systems such as Microsoft Windows and Apple Computer, Inc.'s Mac OS. Until the Web appeared, the Internet itself had been used virtually exclusively by business, scientific, government, and academic professionals rather than by the public at large.

Both Windows 95 and the Web were mileposts on what clearly emerged during the year as the road toward something that industry analysts started calling "convergence." The term pointed toward the coming integration of all forms of information from simple text to moving video as digital data that could be processed, stored, and manipulated by computers using a graphic interface.

By year's end it was clear that PC operating systems, led by Mac OS and Windows 95, had evolved into easy-to-use tools capable of working with converging audio and video material, as well as with the text and photographic images of the past. It also was clear that in the future the medium of exchanging digital information ranging from grocery lists sent via E-mail to full-length Hollywood-type motion pictures would be the World Wide Web. Thus did convergence cross the divide between prediction and reality.

Book publishers were the first of many companies that joined the rush toward convergence in 1995 when it was announced that the entire text of printed works would be available to individual subscribers through the Web, as well as in print sets and in a new CD-ROM version.

Businesses such as computing network giants Oracle Systems Corp. and Novell Inc. began adapting the networks used in corporate computing enterprises to use the same software and communications protocols that made convergence with things such as digital movies possible at the home-entertainment level. Executives and computer scientists at both of these companies, as well as their counterparts all across the industry, increasingly adapted business computer enterprises to operate under the Internet-developed procedures known as Transmission Control Protocol/Internet Protocol (TCP/IP), which was the key technology needed to bring about convergence across computer networks.

TCP/IP can convert any type of data moving from computer to computer via long-distance communications lines into small packets of data that can be transmitted in quick bursts over whatever communications line is available at any given time. For example, one packet, or part of a computer file, might be transmitted from New York City to London by undersea cable, while a second packet is sent via microwave to Los Angeles, Singapore, and Paris before reaching London, depending upon the traffic patterns on the Internet. TCP/ IP thus allow computers to communicate easily, regardless of geographic distances.

Seizing on this power, companies such as Oracle began setting up TCP/IP networks for their business clients to allow customers to reach into the companies' databases from remote points as part of the course of doing business. Such links would allow a company to set up databases to handle product-support calls and to establish systems that would allow remote customers to scan data banks showing what products are in stock and to order them on-line, as well as to perform numerous other efficiencies. Oracle executives noted that the company also set up TCP/IP networks that would allow customer companies to handle their own internal affairs, such as in-house messaging, publishing training materials, and tracking everything from inventory to vacation schedules.

Meanwhile, with Internet computers pervading traditional corporate business environments, 1995 saw a marked acceleration of a trend that surfaced in 1994 as many of the world's leading media companies, including Time Warner Inc., Viacom Inc., and the Walt Disney Co., began forging alliances and consummating mergers with enterprises in the computer and telecommunications industries. Driving the mergers was the clear need of companies with one part of the convergence formula to join forces with companies owning other parts. In each case the combined enterprise was positioned to seize on the opportunities inherent in reducing the totality of the world's information, education, and entertainment content into computer-ready digital form and then selling it through distribution channels pegged to the GUIs of PC operating systems and of the Web.

The largest of the 1995 convergence-related mergers linked the Walt Disney Co. with Capital Cities/ABC, Inc., a $19 billion acquisition plan geared toward a marriage of Capital Cities' holdings in television networks, television stations, cable television systems, newspapers, and radio stations with the huge studios and cable networks used by Disney to produce and sell programming.

Shortly after the Disney-Capital Cities merger was announced, Time Warner announced it would acquire Turner Broadcasting System, Inc., owned by the media magnate Ted Turner Time Warner combined the largest magazine publishing company in the U.S. with Warner Bros. Inc., the world's top producer and distributor of movies and TV programming. Subsidiaries included a major music recording company, book publisher Little, Brown & Co. Inc., and Home Box Office, the largest cable TV movie provider. Time Warner also owned cable television systems that reached nearly 15 million households by the end of 1995. Turner Broadcasting owned the worldwide CNN news organization along with four cable television entertainment networks in the U.S. and four others in Latin America, Asia, and Europe.

Turner also had formed a strategic relationship with the world's leading maker of PC microprocessor chips, Intel Corp., to provide television programming to desktop computers equipped with television circuit boards built by Intel. In November Intel announced that its new chip, the Pentium Pro, would include the ability to serve as a digital television set within the circuitry of every PC equipped with the chip.

The merger mania extended from the media giants into the more traditional computer industry, which saw a wave of mergers, acquisitions, and consolidations that dramatically altered the industry's power structure and dynamics. Apple Computer, which faced increased competition from Windows 95 and from newly released Macintosh clones, remained the subject of takeover rumours.

By far the largest of the completed mergers involved the $3.5 billion acquisition of Lotus Development Corp. by IBM Corp., an alliance that most analysts viewed as a strategy to position IBM, the world's largest computer company, as a participant in the same convergence linking the media companies.

The chief asset of Lotus was an Internet-capable computer networking package called Lotus Notes, designed to let businesses move digital data across multiple types of machines, including IBM's large mainframe computers, mid-range business computers such as IBM's AS/400 and RS/ 6000 lines, and PCs using Windows, Mac OS, IBM's competing OS/2 GUI operating system, and the UNIX operating system long in use by business and academic computing experts. By acquiring Lotus Notes, which worked across multiple computing platforms and was capable of handling the full range of digital content being developed elsewhere, IBM hoped to counter Microsoft, which reigned as the world leader in personal computing, both with its Windows operating system and with a number of projects under development designed to use desktop computers as servers capable of sending cable television programming and movies on demand to other computers linked via the World Wide Web.

Oracle, which previously had focused much of its enterprise toward huge business networks running databases for Fortune 500 companies, took steps to put the company into position as a server of the digital data, such as movies and archived television programs, that the media mergers were geared toward developing and marketing.

In order for virtually all of the other developments to work, however, computers would have to be linked by much faster data-transmission links than the telephone lines that accounted for the great bulk of on-line traffic. There was a strong consensus that achieving this speed was only a matter of time because the technology for the speed needed to send movies along with text down a wire already existed in the form of cable television systems and the fibre-optic cables that phone companies installed in much of the U.S. In fact, much of the merger activity of the year involved owners of these high-bandwidth transmission facilities (such as Time Warner and Capital Cities) joining forces with content providers.

Companies producing the software needed to manage the developing digital communications networks when, and if, they became a reality also benefited from this dynamic. The most visible players were a pair of competing companies, Netscape Communications, Inc., and Spyglass, Inc., both producers of the software called Web servers and Web browsers needed to let people actually use the digital data that came in over their wires to the World Wide Web.

Early in 1995 Microsoft licensed Spyglass' Web browser, Mosaic; changed its name to Microsoft Internet Explorer; and made it the centre of the company's own on-line service, the Microsoft Network. The three largest on-line computer services - America Online, CompuServe, and Prodigy - charged that this Microsoft business initiative gave the company an unfair monopoly because the software needed to access the Microsoft Network was built into the Windows 95 operating system itself.

Netscape, however, proved to be a hugely popular competitor, more than holding its own against Microsoft as some surveys showed that more than 80% of those using the World Wide Web were using Netscape's browser, the Netscape Navigator. Netscape started selling stock to the public in the summer of 1995 and its shares proved to be one of the hottest issues in the history of trading, which thereby underscored the volatility of 1995 computer industry developments. Netscape shares went on sale below $20 each, and a frenzy of trading drove the new issue well above $80 per share within hours. At the close of trading during its first day on the market, Netscape, which had recorded less than $20 million earnings in its entire history, had a market value above $2 billion. This prompted USA Today's editors to note that thanks to excitement over the so-called information superhighway that dominated the 1995 media business scene, Netscape had risen overnight to the point where its market value was greater than that of Maytag Corp. Late in the year, Spyglass announced a stock split to compensate for the quadrupling of its own share price.

INTERNET

It was the year of the Internet's World Wide Web, which by the end of 1996 had so permeated the public's consciousness that even non-technical adults were likely to speak of the "Net" and the "Web." Companies large and small began including a Web-site address in their print advertising and television commercials. Big telecommunications firms began offering their customers Internet access services, competing with America Online, Inc., CompuServe Inc., and hundreds of smaller firms that already did so. Meanwhile, Internet access was no longer limited to computers. New smart telephones were able to send Internet e-mail messages, and televisions equipped with special set-top boxes were able to provide access to the Web.

As a result, some Internet-related companies had a big year in the stock market. Yahoo! Inc., an Internet search engine company that held its initial public stock offering in April, watched its stock rise from the offering price of $13 a share to $33 a share at the close of the next day's trading. It was the most closely watched high-tech public offering since the explosive 1995 debut of Netscape Communications Corp., the Web browser company founded by entrepreneur James Clark and software developer Mark Andreessen.

Profitability, however, eluded most companies doing business on the Internet. While Web-site advertising grew by 83% in the first half of 1996, few commercial business operations on the Internet made money. In fact, most of the advertisers were high-tech companies buying advertising on each other's Web sites. Consumer product companies continued to be cautious about Internet advertising.

Most advertisers tried to capitalize on the Internet's strength - reaching narrowly defined audience groups. There was great interest in extending the Internet to more people. In March U.S. Pres. Bill Clinton participated in a new California school event that spawned subsequent efforts across the country. Called NetDay96, it was a grassroots volunteer campaign to wire schools for Internet access at little cost to the public. By the year's end other states were promoting similar efforts, but the Internet revolution still had not reached many public libraries and schools that could most benefit from easy access to a world of information. An amendment to the Telecommunications Act of 1996 authorized subsidies for information technology to libraries and schools, but late in the year the federal government was just receiving recommendations on how to make that happen.

Some studies suggested the Internet might facilitate learning. The Center for Applied Special Technology, based in Washington, D.C., reported that a study of urban school districts showed that elementary school students with access to the Internet had an advantage in learning over those without access. Its results showed that students who used the Internet scored higher on nine learning criteria, which included greater insight into a topic and accuracy in handling information.

Meanwhile, the major telephone and cable television companies tried to participate in the Internet boom by offering Net access services at previously unheard-of speeds. A new high-speed cable modem that would allow a personal computer (PC) to access the Internet through the same fibre-optic cables that transmitted cable TV programs was introduced in selected cities. It offered access speeds more than 300 times faster than those of most consumer computer modems. Telephone companies spent the closing months of 1996 preparing to introduce "xDSL" transmission technologies, which would allow telephone lines to access the Internet more than 50 times faster than present modems. As the year ended, there were questions about how soon either telephone companies or cable TV companies could introduce the new services to the general population, since in many areas the transmission lines would need to be upgraded before consumers could take advantage of the new services.

Telecommunications reform became more controversial than ever before when the U.S. Congress early in 1996 approved a bill containing the hotly debated

Communications Decency Act. The act provided for fines and jail sentences for Internet content providers who distributed "indecent materials" to minors. In June a three-judge federal panel ruled that the Communications Decency Act was unconstitutional. As part of the opinion, one judge wrote, "As the most participatory form of mass speech yet developed, the Internet deserves the highest protection from governmental intrusion."

That ruling faced federal court appeals, however, and, in the meantime, some states began passing their own restrictive laws governing on-line content. Connecticut, Maryland, New York, and Oklahoma passed laws that restricted the transmission of on-line material. This raised the possibility of widely varied regulations based on geographic boundaries.

Moral questions dogged other media as well. To deal with concerns about the content of television programs, work continued on technology that would allow in-home blocking of certain programs based on a system of ratings. Necessary for such blocking was computer circuitry called the V-chip, which would be built into TV sets.

INDUSTRY'S FINANCIAL TROUBLES

The year 1997 was one in which the computer industry's financial troubles, government investigations, prominent lawsuits, and business consolidations captured as much attention as advancing technology and the continuing growth of the Internet and on-line services. It also was the year in which the U.S. Supreme Court struck down the Communications Decency Act, an attempt to regulate the content of the Internet. The act had been signed by Pres. Bill Clinton in early 1996 in an attempt to protect children from pornography on the Internet, but opponents had claimed the law was so general it could be used to regulate other, more legitimate types of expression. The legislation made it a crime to publish indecent material on the Internet in a way that would make it available to those under 18; violators could receive up to two years in prison and a $250,000 fine. In June the high court threw out the Communications Decency Act on the grounds that it was too broad, vague, and in violation of the Constitution because it "lacks the precision that the First Amendment requires when a statute regulates the content of speech."

COMPUTERS AND SOCIETY

After a year in which Internet access for schools was a top priority, a report by the U.S. Department of Commerce suggested that closing the "digital divide" between technology haves and have-nots would require more than just additional Internet access. Studies showed that minorities, poor people, and residents of rural areas were less likely to have computers, access the Internet, or use new technologies than were whites and those financially better off. The report warned that the digital divide would hurt the ability of minorities to get jobs in areas that required technology skills. It was said, however, that lower prices for PCs had helped bring computing to more lower income families and that federal subsidies had helped bring Internet access to more schools and libraries.

The government issued its rules aimed at protecting children from intrusive Internet marketers. The FTC, acting in response to the Children's Online Privacy Protection Act of 1998, said that Web site operators had to prominently post their privacy polices and set forth what information they collected from children, how that information was used, and whether it was passed on to other people. It also said that parents had to be given access to data collected on their children and be able to have that information deleted if they requested it. The FTC also required Web sites to get verifiable consent from parents before children gave the sites personal information.

COMPUTER CONSUMER TECHNOLOGIES

Digital video (or versatile) disc (DVD) was one of the most talked-about consumer computer technologies in 1996, even though most consumers had not yet seen it. A DVD player would read a shiny disc similar in appearance to a computer CD-ROM but able to hold about 4.7 billion bytes of data, compared with 650 million bytes on a CD-ROM. (Future DVD discs were expected to hold more than eight billion bytes.) The increased DVD storage capacity also would make possible higher-quality video and sound than could be obtained with a videocassette recorder tape and would make it feasible for a moviemaker to sell a single DVD containing several different endings to the same film or multiple versions of the same movie, each in a different language. The first consumer DVD players were expected to debut in the U.S. in early 1997.

Digital photography, a marriage of computer chips and traditional cameras that could capture photos in electronic form, began to trickle into the U.S. market during 1996. These electronic cameras had previously cost from $1,500 to $30,000, but prices had dropped dramatically. Proponents hoped digital cameras costing less than $1,000 would compete for part of the $13 billion that U.S. consumers were expected to spend in 1996 on conventional cameras, photographic accessories, and film processing, while camera manufacturers and computer makers hoped that consumers would be interested in taking digital photos that could be edited on PC screens.

INFORMATION SYSTEMS

The primary vehicles for the purposeful, orchestrated processing of information are information systems - constructs that collect, organize, store, process, and display information in all its forms (raw data, interpreted data, knowledge, and expertise) and formats (text, video, and voice). In principle, any record-keeping system - e.g., an address book or a train schedule - may be regarded as an information system. What sets modern information systems apart is their electronic dimension, which permits extremely fast, automated manipulation of digitally stored data and their transformation from and to analogue representation.

IMPACT OF INFORMATION TECHNOLOGY

Electronic information systems are a phenomenon of the second half of the 20th century. Their evolution is closely tied with advances in two basic technologies: integrated circuits and digital communications.

Integrated circuits are silicon chips containing transistors that store and process information. Advances in the design of these chips, which were first developed in 1958, are responsible for an exponential increase in the cost performance of computer components. For more than two decades the capacity of the basic integrated circuit, the dynamic random-access memory (DRAM) chip, has doubled consistently in intervals of less than two years: from 1,000 transistors (1 kilobit) per chip in 1970 to 1,000,000 (1 megabit) in 1987, 16 megabits in 1993, and 1,000,000,000 (1 gigabit) for the year 2000. A gigabit chip has the capacity of 125,000,000 bytes, approximately equivalent to 14,500 pages, or more than 12 large books volumes.

The speed of microprocessor chips, measured in millions of instructions per second (MIPS), is also increasing near-exponentially: from 10 MIPS in 1985 to 100 MIPS in 1993, with 1,000 MIPS predicted for 1995. By the year 2000 a single chip may process 64 billion instructions per second. If in a particular computing environment in 1993 a chip supported 10 simultaneous users, in the year 2000 such a chip could theoretically support several thousand users.

Full exploitation of these developments for the realm of information systems requires comparable advances in software disciplines. Their major contribution has been to open the use of computer technology to persons other than computer professionals. Interactive applications in the office and home have been made possible by the development of easy-to-use software products for the creation, maintenance, manipulation, and querying of files and records. The database has become a central organizing framework for many information systems, taking advantage of the concept of data independence, which allows data sharing among diverse applications. Database management system (DBMS) software today incorporates high-level programming facilities that do not require one to specify in detail how the data should be processed. The programming discipline as a whole, however, progresses in an evolutionary manner. Whereas semiconductor field advances are measured by orders of magnitude, the writing and understanding of large suites of software that characterize complex information systems progress more slowly. The complexity of the data processes that comprise very large information systems has so far eluded major breakthroughs, and the cost-effectiveness of the software development sector improves only gradually.

The utility of computers is vastly augmented by their ability to communicate with one another, so as to share data and its processing. Local-area networks (LANs) permit the sharing of data, programs, printers, and electronic mail within offices and buildings. In wide-area networks, such as the Internet, which connect thousands of computers around the globe, computer-to-computer communication uses a variety of media as transmission lines--electric-wire audio circuits, coaxial cables, radio and microwaves (as in satellite communication), and, most recently, optical fibres. The latter are replacing coaxial cable in the Integrated Services Digital Network (ISDN), which is capable of carrying digital information in the form of voice, text, and video simultaneously. To communicate with another machine, a computer requires data circuit-terminating equipment, or DCE, which connects it to the transmission line. When an analogue line such as a dial-up telephone line is used, the DCE is called a modem (for modulator/demodulator); it also provides the translation of the digital signal to analogue and vice versa. By using data compression, the relatively inexpensive high-speed modems currently in use can transmit data at speeds of more than 100 kilobits per second. When digital lines are used, the DCE allows substantially higher speeds; for instance, the U.S. scholarly network NSFNET, set up by the National Science Foundation, transmits information at 45 million bits per second. The National Research and Education Network, proposed by the U.S. government in 1991, is designed to send data at speeds in the gigabit-per-second range, comfortably moving gigantic volumes of text, video, and sound across a web of digital highways.

Computer networks are complex entities. Each network operates according to a set of procedures called the network protocol. The proliferation of incompatible protocols during the early 1990s has been brought under relative control by the Open Systems Interconnection (OSI) reference Model formulated by the International Organization for Standardization. To the extent that individual protocols conform to the OSI recommendations, computer networks can now be interconnected efficiently through gateways.

Computer networking facilitates the current trend toward distributed information systems. At the corporate level, the central database may be distributed over a number of computer systems in different locations, yet its querying and updating are carried out simultaneously against the composite database. An individual searching for public-access information can traverse disparate computer networks to peruse hundreds of autonomous databases and within seconds or minutes download a copy of the desired document into a personal workstation.

The future of information systems may be gleaned from several areas of current research. As all information carriers (text, video, and sound) can be converted to digital form and manipulated by increasingly sophisticated techniques, the ranges of media, functions, and capabilities of information systems are constantly expanding. Evolving techniques of natural-language processing and understanding, knowledge representation, and neural process modelling have begun to join the more traditional repertoire of methods of content analysis and manipulation.

The use of these techniques opens the possibility of eliciting new knowledge from existing data, such as the discovery of a previously unknown medical syndrome or of a causal relationship in a disease. Computer visualization, a new field that has grown expansively since the early 1990s, deals with the conversion of masses of data emanating from instruments, databases, or computer simulations into visual displays - the most efficient method of human information reception, analysis, and exchange.

Related to computer visualization is the research area of virtual reality or virtual worlds, which denotes the generation of synthetic environments through the use of three-dimensional displays and interaction devices. A number of research directions in this area are particularly relevant to future information systems: knowledge-based world modelling; the development of physical analogues for abstract quantitative and organizational data; and search and retrieval in large virtual worlds. The cumulative effect of these new research areas is a gradual transformation of the role of information systems from that of data processing to that of cognition aiding.

Present-day computers are remarkably versatile machines capable of assisting humans in nearly every problem-solving task that involves symbol manipulations. Television, on the other hand, has penetrated societies throughout the world as a non-interactive display device for combined video and audio signals. The impending convergence of three digital technologies - namely, the computer, very-high-definition television (V-HDTV), and ISDN data communications - is all but inevitable. In such a system, a large-screen multimedia display monitor, containing a 64-megabit primary memory and a billion-byte hard disk for data storage and playback, would serve as a computer and, over ISDN fibre links, an interactive television receiver.

ANALYSIS AND DESIGN OF SYSTEMS

The building of information systems falls within the domain of engineering. As is true with other engineering disciplines, the nature and tools of information systems engineering are evolving owing to both technological developments and better perceptions of societal needs for information services. Early information systems were designed to be operated by information professionals, and they frequently did not attain their stated social purpose. Modern information systems are increasingly used by persons who have little or no previous hands-on experience with information technology but who possess a much better perception about what this technology should accomplish in their professional and personal environments. A correct understanding of the requirements, preferences, and "information styles" of these end users is crucial to the design and success of today's information systems.

The methodology involved in building an information system consists of a set of iterative activities that are cumulatively referred to as the system's life cycle

The principal objective of the systems analysis phase is the specification of what the system is required to do. In the systems design phase such specifications are converted to a hierarchy of increasingly detailed charts that define the data required and decompose the processes to be carried out on data to a level at which they can be expressed as instructions of a computer program. The systems development phase consists of writing and testing computer software and of developing data input and output forms and conventions. Systems implementation is the installation of a physical system and the activities it entails, such as the training of operators and users. Systems maintenance refers to the further evolution of the functions and structure of a system that result from changing requirements and technologies, experience with the system's use, and fine-tuning of its performance.

Many information systems are implemented with generic, "off-the-shelf" software rather than with custom-built programs; versatile database management software and its nonprocedural programming languages fit the needs of small and large systems alike. The development of large systems that cannot use off-the-shelf software is an expensive, time-consuming, and complex undertaking. Prototyping, an interactive session in which users confirm a system's proposed functions and features early in the design stage, is a practice intended to raise the probability of success of such an undertaking. Some of the tools of computer-aided software engineering available to the systems analyst and designer verify the logic of systems design, automatically generate a program code from low-level specifications, and automatically produce software and system specifications.

The eventual goal of information systems engineering is to develop software "factories" that use natural language and artificial intelligence techniques as part of an integrated set of tools to support the analysis and design of large information systems.

SIMULATION

Computers have had a dramatic impact on the management of industrial production systems and the fields of operations research and industrial engineering. The speed and data-handling capabilities of computers allow engineers and scientists to build larger, more realistic models of organized systems and to get meaningful solutions to those models through the use of simulation techniques.

Simulation consists of calculating the performance of a system by evaluating a model of it for randomly selected values of variables contained within it. Most simulation in operations research is concerned with "stochastic" variables; that is, variables whose values change randomly within some probability distribution over time. The random sampling employed in simulation requires either a supply of random numbers or a procedure for generating them. It also requires a way of converting these numbers into the distribution of the relevant variable, a way of sampling these values, and a way of evaluating the resulting performance.

A simulation in which decision making is performed by one or more real decision makers is called "operational gaming." Such simulations are commonly used in the study of interactions of decision makers as in competitive situations. Military gaming has long been used as a training device, but only relatively recently has it been used for research purposes. There is still considerable difficulty, however, in drawing inferences from operational games to the real world.

Experimental optimization is a means of experimenting on a system so as to find the best solution to a problem within it. Such experiments conducted either simultaneously or sequentially, may be designed in various ways, no one of which is best in all situations.

OPERATIONS RESEARCH

Operations research attempts to provide those who manage organized systems with an objective and quantitative basis for decision; it is normally carried out by teams of scientists and engineers drawn from a variety of disciplines. Thus, operations research is not a science itself but rather the application of science to the solution of managerial and administrative problems, and it focuses on the performance of organized systems taken as a whole rather than on their parts taken separately. Usually concerned with systems in which human behaviour plays an important part, operations research differs in this respect from systems engineering, which, using a similar approach tends to concentrate on systems in which human behaviour is not important. Operations research was originally concerned with improving the operations of existing systems rather than developing new ones; the converse was true of systems engineering. This difference, however, has been disappearing as both fields have matured.

The subject matter of operations research consists of decisions that control the operations of systems. Hence, it is concerned with how managerial decisions are and should be made, how to acquire and process data and information required to make decisions effectively, how to monitor decisions once they are implemented, and how to organize the decision-making and decision-implementation process. Extensive use is made of older disciplines such as logic, mathematics, and statistics, as well as more recent scientific developments such as communications theory, decision theory, cybernetics, organization theory, the behavioural sciences, and general systems theory.

In the 19th century the Industrial Revolution involved mechanization or replacement of human by machine as a source of physical work. Study and improvement of such work formed the basis of the field of industrial engineering. Many contemporary issues are concerned with automation or mechanization of mental work. The primary technologies involved are mechanization of symbol generation (observation by machines such as radar and sonar), mechanization of symbol transmission (communication by telephone, radio, and television), and mechanization of logical manipulation of symbols (data processing and decision making by computer). Operations research applies the scientific method to the study of mental work and provides the knowledge and understanding required to make effective use of personnel and machines to carry it out.

COMPUTERS AND SYSTEMS ENGINEERING

Systems engineering also profited from the advent of computers and the subsequent development of powerful, high-level programming languages, which affected the field in two principal ways. First, they provided new tools for analyzing complex systems by means of extensive calculations or direct simulation. In the second place, they could be used to digest large amounts of data or as actual constituents of complex systems, especially those concerned largely with information transmission. This opened up the possibility of processing information as well as simply transmitting it in such systems.

Impact of military weapons problems on systems engineering began soon after World War II. A landmark date was 1945, when the development of Nike Ajax, a U.S. air defence missile system, was initiated.

In 1945 available rocket propulsion seemed barely sufficient to give the missile a satisfactory tactical range. It was discovered that achievable range depended on several parameters, such as the weight and size of the warhead, fineness of the missile's aerodynamic design, degree of manoeuvrability provided by the control system, and shape of the trajectory and average speed along it. Thus an effective systems engineering effort was mounted in which a variety of combinations of the missile's properties were explored, with the objective of achieving the best balance between range and other tactical characteristics.

Control and feedback questions were also important aspects of the overall systems problem. The whole system was in fact a gigantic feedback loop because the missile was controlled by orders sent it from a ground computer, and the computer input included information on what the tracking radar observed the missile to be doing. Thus there was a closed feedback loop from missile to computer and back to the missile again. There were also such subsidiary feedback loops as that of the autopilot controlling the attitude of the missile, and the dynamic response of the system was further affected by the need to process the radar signals to remove radar "jitter." The analysis of such elaborate dynamical systems involving interlaced feedback paths has become an important special part of the general systems area.

In the 1950s and 1960s systems engineering also grew in other directions, largely as a result of weapons systems projects associated with the Cold War. Thus the Ajax study was concerned with the dynamics of a single isolated missile. On the other hand, the defence systems that grew up in the 1950s involved the coordinated operation of a large number of missiles, guns, interceptors, and radar installations scattered over a considerable area. These were all held together by a large digital computer, which thus became the central element of the system. The SAGE (semi-automatic ground environment) system in the United States is a good example.

During the same years the systems approach also became increasingly identified with management functions. Thus the phrase "systems engineering and technical direction" came into use to describe the role of a systems engineer responsible for both the initial planning of a project and its subsequent management. So-called planning, programming, and budgeting (PPB) techniques were developed to provide similar combinations of systems engineering and financial management.

In non-military fields systems engineering has developed along similar though more modest lines. Early applications were likely to stress feedback control systems in large-scale automated production facilities, such as steel-rolling mills and petroleum refineries. Later applications stressed computer-based management information and control systems somewhat like those that had earlier been developed for air defence. In more recent years the systems approach has occasionally been applied to much larger civilian enterprises, such as the planning of new cities.

Societies were organized, beginning with the Operational Research Club of Britain, formed in 1948, which in 1954 became the Operational Research Society. The Operations Research Society in America was formed in 1952. Many other national societies appeared; the first international conference on operations research was held at Oxford University in 1957. In 1959 an International Federation of Operational Research Societies was formed.

Three essential characteristics of operations research are a systems orientation, the use of interdisciplinary teams, and the application of scientific method to the conditions under which the research is conducted.

SYSTEMS ORIENTATION

The systems approach to problems recognises that the behaviour of any part of a system has some effect on the behaviour of the system as a whole. Even if the individual components are performing well, however, the system as a whole is not necessarily performing equally well. For example, assembling the best of each type of automobile part, regardless of make, does not necessarily result in a good automobile or even one that will run, because the parts may not fit together. It is the interaction between parts, and not the actions of any single part, that determines how well a system performs.

Thus, operations research attempts to evaluate the effect of changes in any part of a system on the performance of the system as a whole and to search for causes of a problem that arises in one part of a system in other parts or in the interrelationships between parts. In industry, a production problem may be approached by a change in marketing policy. For example, if a factory fabricates a few profitable products in large quantities and many less profitable items in small quantities, long efficient production runs of high-volume, high-profit items may have to be interrupted for short runs of low-volume, low-profit items. An operations researcher might propose reducing the sales of the less profitable items and increasing those of the profitable items by placing salesmen on an incentive system that especially compensates them for selling particular items.

COMPUTER INTEGRATED MANUFACTURING

Computers have come to be used in all stages of manufacture: design, scheduling, management, manufacturing, and testing. The integration of these phases of computer involvement is called computer-integrated manufacturing.

AUTOMOTIVE INDUSTRY

Computers are involved (as CAD systems) not only in the design of cars but also in the manufacturing and testing process, perhaps making use of CIM technology. Today's automobiles include numerous computer chips that analyze sensor data and alert the driver to actual and potential malfunctions. For example, the antilock braking system (ABS) is computer controlled. Other computers provide warnings of actual and potential malfunctions. Automobile manufacturers are developing safer, "smart" airbags and remote tire-pressure monitors. Although increased reliability has been achieved by implementing such computerisation, a drawback is that only automotive repair shops with a large investment in high-tech interfaces and diagnostic tools for these computerized systems can handle any but the simplest repairs.

CONCEPT FORMATION BY MACHINE

Computers can be programmed to process information and to develop classification rules (e.g., they can play chess and make decisions about business or military problems). Essentially such devices are programmed to mimic the process of problem solving required of subjects in laboratory experiments on concept learning. In this sense, machines have formed concepts; but their functions remain relatively impoverished.

Efficient linguistic behaviour has proven particularly difficult to produce in a machine, despite numerous attempts. Yet there is no evidence that human concept formation is based on any mode of handling information that in principle could not be built into a machine. It is almost an article of faith among many investigators that human thinking can be explained mechanistically in physiological terms, but the scientists themselves do not yet seem to have developed concepts adequate for producing machines that can approach the full range of human talent.

COMPUTER GRAPHICS

This refers to the use of computers to produce pictorial images. The images produced can be printed documents or animated motion pictures, but the term computer graphics refers particularly to images displayed on a video display screen, or display monitor. These screens can display graphic as well as alphanumeric data. A computer-graphics system basically consists of a computer to store and manipulate images, a display screen, various input and output devices, and a graphics software package - i.e., a program that enables a computer to process graphic images by means of mathematical language. These programs enable the computer to draw, colour, shade, and manipulate the images held in its memory.

A computer displays images on the phosphor-coated surface of a graphics display screen by means of an electron beam that sweeps the screen many times each second. Those portions of the screen energised by the beam emit light, and changes in the intensity of the beam determine their brightness and hue. The brightness of the resulting image fades quickly, however, and must be continuously "refreshed" by the beam, typically 30 times per second.

Graphics software programs enable a user to draw, colour, shade, and manipulate an image on a display screen with commands input by a keyboard. A picture can be drawn or redrawn onto the screen with the use of a mouse, a pressure-sensitive tablet, or a light pen. Pre-existing images on paper can be scanned into the computer through the use of scanners, digitizers, pattern-recognition devices, or digital cameras. Frames of images on videotape also can be entered into a computer. Various output devices have been developed as well; special programs send digital data from the computer's memory to an image-setter or film recorder, which prints the image on paper or on photographic film. The computer can also generate hard copy by means of plotters and laser or dot-matrix printers.

Pictures are stored and processed in a computer's memory by either of two methods: raster graphics and vector graphics. Raster-type graphics maintain an image as a matrix of independently controlled dots, while vector graphics maintain it as a collection of points, lines, and arcs. Raster graphics are now the dominant computer graphics technology.

In raster graphics, the computer's memory stores an image as a matrix, or grid, of individual dots, or pixels (picture elements). Each pixel is encoded in the computer's memory as one or several bits - i.e., binary digits represented by 0 or 1. A 2-bit pixel can represent either black or white, while a 4-bit pixel can represent any of 16 different colours or shades of grey. The constituent bits that encode a picture in the computer's memory are called a bit map. Computers need large processing and memory capacities to translate the enormous amounts of information contained in a picture into the digital code of a bit map, and graphics software programs use special algorithms (computational processes) to perform these procedures.

In raster graphics, the thousands of tiny pixels that make up an individual image are projected onto a display screen as illuminated dots that from a distance appear as a contiguous image. The picture frame consists of hundreds of tiny horizontal rows, each of which contains hundreds of pixels. An electron beam creates the grid of pixels by tracing each horizontal line from left to right, one pixel at a time, from the top line to the bottom line.

Raster graphics create uniform coloured areas and distinct patterns and allow precise manipulation because their constituent images can be altered one dot at a time. Their main disadvantage is that the images are subtly stair-cased - i.e., diagonal lines and edges appear jagged and less distinct when viewed from a very short distance. A corollary of television technology, raster graphics emerged in the early 1970s and had largely displaced vector systems by the '90s.

In vector graphics, images are made up of a series of lines, each of which is stored in the computer's memory as a vector - i.e., as two points on an x-y matrix. On a vector-type display screen, an electron beam sweeps back and forth between the points designated by the computer and the paths so energized emit light, thereby creating lines; solid shapes are created by grouping lines closely enough to form a contiguous image. Vector-graphics technology was developed in the mid-1960s and widely used until it was supplanted by raster graphics. Its application is now largely restricted to highly linear work in computer-aided design and architectural drafting, and even this is performed on raster-type screens with the vectors converted into dots.

Computer graphics have found widespread use in printing, product design and manufacturing, scientific research, and entertainment since the 1960s. In the business office, computers routinely create graphs and tables to illustrate text information. Computer-aided design systems have replaced drafting boards in the design of a vast array of products ranging from buildings to automotive bodies and aircraft hulls to electrical and electronic devices.

Computers are also often used to test various mechanical, electrical, or thermal properties of the component under design. Scientists use computers to simulate the behaviour of complicated natural systems in animated motion-picture sequences. These pictorial visualizations can afford a clearer understanding of the multiple forces or variables at work in such phenomena as nuclear and chemical reactions, large-scale gravitational interactions, hydraulic flow, load deformation, and physiological systems. Computer graphics are nowhere as visible as in the entertainment industry, which uses them to create the interactive animations of video games and the special effects in motion pictures. Computers have also come into increasing use in commercial illustration and in the digitalization of images for use in CD-ROM products, online services, and other electronic media.

MATHEMATICAL PROGRAMMING

This is a theoretical tool of management science and economics in which management operations are described by mathematical equations that can be manipulated for a variety of purposes. It is used on problems for which calculus is unsuitable. If the basic descriptions involved take the form of linear algebraic equations, the technique is described as linear programming. If more complex forms are required, the term non-linear programming is applied. Mathematical programming is used in planning production schedules, in transportation, in military logistics, and in calculating economic growth, by inserting assumed values for the variables in the equations and solving for the unknowns. Computers are widely used in arriving at solutions.

MATHEMATICAL AND STATISTICAL ANALYSIS

Although the use of mathematics in geography is ancient, the extensive and fundamental utilization of quantitative and statistical methods in modern geography arose mainly in the second half of the 20th century. The methodologies are similar to or identical with those used in the physical, biological, and social sciences, except that special attention is given to the problems of place-specific or area-specific data, in which the recognition and description of spatial patterns require special techniques. Model building, probability theory, and simulation techniques have proved to be of special value. Torsten Hägerstrand, for example, utilized an excellent data base in his native Sweden to make his seminal studies of the geographic diffusion of innovations. The development of electronic computers greatly expanded the power to analyse geographic problems.

Computers can store immense amounts of data, and they greatly accelerate the speed at which complicated statistical and mathematical problems can be solved. They have become particularly valuable for their ability to handle such programs as those that measure spatial contiguity, spatial diffusion through time, and locational patterns, as well as for their use in network analysis, node accessibility indexes, map projections, and the display of cartographic data.

There is a long-standing tradition in geography of placing special value on direct field observation and mapping. Much geographic knowledge is based on observations, if not by a research investigator directly then by others who write about observations revealed in oral interviews, in census enumerations, or in the interpretation of remote sensing images, aerial photographs, or maps. The questions others ask may not be formulated in such a way as to reveal the locational characteristics and spatial patterns so important to the geographer. Census information, for example, often fails to be broken into units small enough to permit satisfactory aerial analysis. Thus, geographers often need to gather their own data.

CINEMATOGRAPHIC TECHNOLOGY

Efforts to lessen the extraordinary labour and costs of animation have taken two basic directions: simplification and computerization. Inexpensive cartoons made for television have often resorted to "limited animation," in which each drawing is repeated anywhere from two to five times. The resultant movements are jerky, rather than smoothly gradated. Often only part of the body is animated, and the background and the remaining parts of the figure do not change at all. Another shortcut is "cycling," whereby only a limited number of phases of body movement are drawn and then repeated to create more complicated movements such as walking or talking.

Although computers can be used to create the limited animation described above, they can also be used in virtually every step of sophisticated animation. Computers have been used, for example, to automate the movement of the rostrum camera or to supply the in-between drawings for full animation. If a three-dimensional figure is translated into computer terms (i.e., digitised), the computer can move or rotate the object convincingly through space. Hence, computer animation can demonstrate highly complex movements for medical or other scientific researchers.

Animators who work with computers usually distinguish between computer-assisted animation, which uses computers to facilitate some stages of the laborious production process, and computer-generated animation, which creates imagery through mathematical or computer language rather than through photography or drawing. Finally, computers may be used to modify or enhance a drawing that has been initiated in the traditional manner.

WARNING SYSTEM

In the second half of the 20th century, warning against ballistic missiles with nuclear warheads has taken precedence over all other warning systems. Large ground radars, operating in the very high frequency (VHF) or ultrahigh frequency (UHF) range, are used. The radars search the skies and track detected objects. Computers calculate trajectory to determine if the target is a missile or an Earth-orbiting object. Depending on the trajectory, the number of objects, and other criteria, alerts, tentative warnings, or all-out warning signals are transmitted to command centres.

Surface-based radars have one serious flaw: they can detect an object only after it appears above the Earth's horizon. For earlier warning, over-the-horizon radars or satellite-borne infrared detectors can be used.

There are two types of over-the-horizon radars, operating in the high frequency range, which can reflect from the ionosphere. One system, called forward scatter, transmits from one location and receives the signal several thousand miles away on the other side of the launch point. The back-scatter system receives the signal from the same location as the transmitter, as is done in conventional radar. Both systems detect variations in the received signal due to fluctuations in the ionosphere caused by the missile's exhaust plume as it traverses the ionosphere.

TEACHING MACHINE

This refers to any mechanical device used for presenting a program of instructional material.

There are many types of teaching machines. In general, they all work on the same method, which is to present a question, have the user indicate the answer, and then provide the user with the correct answer. Some machines may be extremely simple, such as test sheets or books so programmed that the student locates the answers to the questions later. For instance, a book may pose a series of questions, provide spaces for the answers, and then give the correct answers on a different page. Another device may use a plastic cover to hide all but the question and the space for an answer; when the question is answered, the cover is pulled down to reveal the correct answer and the next question. One type uses chemically treated paper so that if the correct answer to a question is marked, the paper turns colour. A more complicated machine presents multiple-choice questions in a window, with various keys to press to indicate the correct answer. The following question appears only if the correct answer was chosen. Computers and the recording equipment used in foreign language laboratories are examples of teaching machines.

All teaching machines depend on a program, that is, a series of questions presented that provide a student with a certain amount of challenge as well as a chance to learn. There are many advantages to the use of teaching machines. They are particularly useful in subjects that require drill, such as arithmetic or a foreign language. Users can proceed at their own pace and also have an opportunity to review their work. If the machines are used in a classroom, they relieve teachers of some of the time-consuming aspects of drilling students, allowing them to give more attention to individuals with specific problems or to concentrate on some particularly difficult area of instruction.

TELESCOPE AND COMPUTER

Besides the telescope itself, the electronic computer has become the astronomer's most important tool. Indeed, the computer has revolutionised the use of the telescope to the point where the collection of observational data is now completely automated. The astronomer need only identify the object to be observed, and the rest is carried out by the computer and auxiliary electronic equipment.

A telescope can be set to observe automatically by means of electronic sensors appropriately placed on the telescope axis. Precise quartz or atomic clocks send signals to the computer, which in turn activates the telescope sensors to collect data at the proper time. The computer not only makes possible more efficient use of telescope time but also permits a more detailed analysis of the data collected than could have been done manually. Data analysis that would have taken a lifetime or longer to complete with a mechanical calculator can now be done within hours or even minutes with a high-speed computer.

Improved means of recording and storing computer data also have contributed to astronomical research. Optical disc data storage technology, such as the CD-ROM (compact disc read-only memory) or the WORM (write-once read-many) disc has provided astronomers with the ability to store and retrieve vast amounts of telescopic and other astronomical data. A 12-centimetre CD-ROM, for example, may hold up to 600 megabytes of data--the equivalent of 20 nine-track magnetic tapes or 1,500 floppy discs. A 13-centimetre WORM disc typically holds about 300 to 400 megabytes of data.

REAL-TIME SYSTEMS

The design of real-time systems is becoming increasingly important. Computers have been incorporated into cars, aircraft, manufacturing assembly lines, and other applications to control processes as they occur - known as "in real time." It is not practical in such instances to provide input to the computer, allow it to compute for some indefinite length of time, and then examine the output. The computer output must be available in a timely fashion, and the processor (or processors) must be carefully chosen and the tasks specially scheduled so that deadlines are met. Frequently, real-time tasks repeat at fixed time intervals; for example, every so many seconds, sensor data are gathered and analysed and a control signal generated. In such cases, scheduling theory is utilized by the systems designer in determining how the tasks should be scheduled on a given processor.

A good example of a system that requires real-time action is the antilock braking system (ABS) on most newer vehicles; because it is critical that the ABS instantly react to brake-pedal pressure and begin a program of pumping the brakes, such an application is said to have a hard deadline. Some other real-time systems are said to have soft deadlines, in that, although it is deemed important to meet them, no disaster will happen if the system's response is slightly delayed; an example is ocean shipping and tracking systems.

The concept of "best effort" arises in real-time system design, not only because soft deadlines may sometimes be slipped, but because hard deadlines may sometimes be met by computing a less than optimal result. For example, most details on an air traffic controller's screen are approximations - e.g., altitude, which need not be displayed to the nearest inch - that do not interfere with air safety.

DATA ENCRYPTION

Also called ENCRYPTION, OR ENCIPHERMENT, the process of disguising information as "ciphertext," or data unintelligible to an unauthorized person. Conversely, decryption, or decipherment, is the process of converting ciphertext back into its original format. Manual encryption has been used since the ancient Greek times, but the term has become associated with the disguising of information via electronic computers. Encryption is a process basic to cryptology.

Computers encrypt data by applying an algorithm - i.e., a set of procedures or instructions for performing a specified task - to a block of data. A personal encryption key, or name, known only to the transmitter of the message and its intended receiver, is used to control the algorithm's encryption of the data, thus yielding unique ciphertext that can be decrypted only by using the key.

Since the late 1970s, two types of encryption have emerged. Conventional symmetric encryption requires the same key for both encryption and decryption. A common symmetric encryption system is the Data Encryption Standard (DES), an extremely complex algorithm approved as a standard by the U.S. National Bureau of Standards.

Asymmetric encryption, or public-key cryptography, requires a pair of keys; one for encryption and one for decryption. It allows disguised data to be transferred between allied parties at different locations without also having to transfer the (not encrypted) key. A common asymmetric encryption standard is the RSA (Rivest-Shamir-Adleman) algorithm.

Encryption keys selected at random and of sufficient length are considered almost impregnable. A key, 10 characters long selected from the 256 available ASCII characters could take roughly 40 billion centuries to decode, assuming that the perpetrator was attempting 10,000 different keys per second.

CO-ORDINATING AND MANAGING LOGISTICS

The individual elements of a firm's logistics system must be tied together. The firm's management may have a separate logistics department that is equal in status with other major departments such as finance, production, marketing, and so on. However, most firms are more likely to have these functions spread throughout various departments loosely coordinated by a logistics staff. (A more traditional firm had its logistics activities associated with inbound and interplant movements handled by the production staff, and these activities grouped were known as "materials management." The traditional firm's logistics activities involving outbound products leaving the assembly line and bound for customers were handled by the marketing staff, and these activities grouped were known as "physical distribution management.") Today, some firms rely on "third-party" logistics, wherein they contract with an outside firm to coordinate, manage, and sometimes perform the various functions.

The second way that logistics activities are linked is by communications. In recent years, improved communications have taken the place of inventory. Some chain stores have scanners at checkout counters where a customer buys merchandise. These scanners are linked directly to the chain's home office so that it has instantaneous information as to what is being sold. Knowing this, they can restock the store and intermediate channels immediately, rather than having a large inventory at that store in anticipation of what might sell.

Third, control systems help link the elements of logistics systems. The reason for this is that the goods moving through a system are valuable and therefore are targets for pilferage by employees or organized thefts conducted by outsiders. Hence, a logistics system needs a control system that tracks the goods as they move from place to place to ensure that some do not disappear. The system is designed so that when goods do leave the system, they must be exchanged for proper documentation or payment. Computers also help link a firm's logistics activities. As of 1992, more than 1,500 different computer software packages were available for use by logistics managers.

PHOTONIC MATERIALS

Computers and communications systems have been dominated by electronic technology since their beginnings, but photonic technology is making serious inroads throughout the information movement and management systems with such devices as lasers, light-emitting diodes, photo-detecting diodes, optical switches, optical amplifiers, optical modulators, and optical fibres. Indeed, for long-distance terrestrial and transoceanic transmission of information, photonics has almost completely displaced electronics.

CRYSTALLINE MATERIALS

The light detectors and generators listed above are actually optoelectronic, because they link photonic and electronic systems. They employ the III-V compound semiconductors described above, many of them characterized by their band gaps - i.e., the energy minimum of the electron conduction band and the energy maximum of hole valence bands occur at the same location in the momentum space, allowing electrons and holes to recombine and radiate photons efficiently. (By contrast, the conduction band minimum and the valence band maximum in silicon have dissimilar momenta, and therefore the electrons and holes cannot recombine efficiently.) Among the important compounds are gallium arsenide, aluminum gallium arsenide, indium gallium arsenide phosphide, indium phosphide, and aluminum indium arsenide.

Fabricating a single crystal from these combinations of elements is far more difficult than creating a single crystal of electronic-grade silicon. Special furnaces are required, and the process can take several days. Notwithstanding the precision involved, the sausage-shaped boule is less than half the diameter of a silicon ingot and is subject to a much higher rate of defects. Researchers are continuously seeking ways to reduce the thermal stresses that are primarily responsible for dislocations in the III-V crystal lattice that cause these defects. The purity and structural perfection of the final single-crystal substrates affect the qualities of the crystalline layers that are grown on them and the regions that are diffused or implanted in them during the manufacture of photonic devices.

AEROPLANES AND COMPUTERS

Since the mid-1960s, computer technology has been continually developed to the point at which aircraft and engine designs can be simulated and tested in myriad variations under a full spectrum of environmental conditions prior to construction. As a result, practical consideration may be given to a series of aircraft configurations, which, while occasionally and usually unsuccessfully attempted in the past, can now be used in production aircraft. These include forward swept wings, canard surfaces, blended body and wings, and the refinement of specialized airfoils (wing, propeller, and turbine blade). With this goes a far more comprehensive understanding of structural requirements, so that adequate strength can be maintained even as reductions are made in weight.

Complementing and enhancing the results of the use of computers in design is the pervasive use of computers on board the aircraft itself. Computers are used to test and calibrate the aircraft's equipment, so that, both before and during flight, potential problems can be anticipated and corrected. Whereas the first autopilots were devices that simply maintained an aircraft in straight and level flight, modern computers permit an autopilot system to guide an aircraft from takeoff to landing, incorporating continuous adjustment for wind and weather conditions and ensuring that fuel consumption is minimized. In the most advanced instances, the role of the pilot has been changed from that of an individual who continuously controlled the aircraft in every phase of flight to a systems manager who oversees and directs the human and mechanical resources in the cockpit.

The use of computers for design and in-flight control is synergistic, for more radical designs can be created when there are on-board computers to continuously adapt the controls to flight conditions. The degree of inherent stability formerly desired in an aircraft design called for the wing, fuselage, and empennage (tail assembly) of what came to be conventional size and configurations, with their inherent weight and drag penalties. By using computers that can sense changes in flight conditions and make corrections hundreds and even thousands of times a second - far faster and more accurately than any pilot's capability - aircraft can be deliberately designed to be unstable. Wings can, if desired, be given a forward sweep, and tail surfaces can be reduced in size to an absolute minimum (or, in a flying wing layout, eliminated completely). Airfoils can be customized not only for a particular aircraft's wing or propeller but also for particular points on those components.

COMPUTER EXTENSION OF CHESS THEORY

Computers have played a role in extending the knowledge of chess. In 1986 Kenneth Thompson of AT&T Bell Laboratories reported a series of discoveries in basic endgames. By working backward from positions of checkmate, Thompson was able to build up an enormous number of variations showing every possible way of reaching the final ones. This has been possible with only the most elementary endgames, with no more than five pieces on the board. Thompson's research proved that certain conclusions that had remained unchallenged in endgame books for decades were untrue. For example, with best play on both sides, a king and queen can defeat a king and two bishops in 92.1 percent of the initial starting positions; this endgame had been regarded as a hopeless drawn situation. Also, a king and two bishops can defeat a king and lone knight in 91.8 percent of situations--despite human analysis that concluded the position was drawn. Thompson's research of some five-piece endgames required considering more than 121 million positions.

Because of their ability to store information, computers had become invaluable to professional players by the 1990s, particularly in the analysis of adjourned games. However, computers have severe limits. In the 1995 PCA championship, Kasparov won the 10th game with a heavily analysed opening based on the sacrifice of a rook. According to his aides, the prepared idea was tested on a computer beforehand, and the program evaluated the variation as being in the opponent's favour until it had reached the end of Kasparov's lengthy analysis.

The availability of top-notch microcomputers poses a major problem for postal chess. A principal difference between over-the-board chess and all forms of correspondence chess is that in the latter players are permitted to analyze a position by moving the pieces and by consulting reference books. By the 1990s most serious postal players used a computer database containing thousands of games categorized by opening moves. However, if the use of computers is extended to finding the best moves in the middle-game or endgame, postal chess becomes computer chess. The International Correspondence Chess Federation said in 1993 that "the existence of chess computers is a reality and for correspondence chess the use of chess computers cannot be controlled."

COMPUTER-ASSISTED INSTRUCTION

This is a program of instructional material presented by means of a computer or computer systems.

The use of computers in education started in the 1960s. With the advent of convenient microcomputers in the 1970s, computer use in schools has become widespread from primary education through the university level and even in some preschool programs. Instructional computers are basically used in one of two ways: either they provide a straightforward presentation of data or they fill a tutorial role in which the student is tested on comprehension.

If the computer has a tutorial program, the student is asked a question by the computer; the student types in an answer and then gets an immediate response to the answer. If the answer is correct, the student is routed to more challenging problems; if the answer is incorrect, various computer messages will indicate the flaw in procedure, and the program will bypass more complicated questions until the student shows mastery in that area.

There are many advantages to using computers in educational instruction. They provide one-to-one interaction with a student, as well as an instantaneous response to the answers elicited, and allow students to proceed at their own pace. Computers are particularly useful in subjects that require drill, freeing teacher time from some classroom tasks so that a teacher can devote more time to individual students. A computer program can be used diagnostically, and, once a student's problem has been identified, it can then focus on the problem area. Finally, because of the privacy and individual attention afforded by a computer, some students are relieved of the embarrassment of giving an incorrect answer publicly or of going more slowly through lessons than other classmates.

There are drawbacks to the implementation of computers in instruction, however. They are generally costly systems to purchase, maintain, and update. There are also fears, whether justified or not, that the use of computers in education decreases the amount of human interaction.

One of the more difficult aspects of instructional computers is the availability and development of software, or computer programs. Courseware can be bought as a fully developed package from a software company, but the program provided this way may not suit the particular needs of the individual class or curriculum. A courseware template may be purchased, which provides a general format for tests and drill instruction, with the individual particulars to be inserted by the individual school system or teacher. The disadvantage to this system is that instruction tends to be boring and repetitive, with tests and questions following the same pattern for every course. Software can be developed in-house, that is, a school, course, or teacher could provide the courseware exactly tailored to its own needs, but this is expensive, time-consuming, and may require more programming expertise than is available.

DIGITAL ELECTRONICS

Reference was made earlier to digital forms of communication. These arose largely because of the way computers operate - i.e., by using digital representations of numbers. Computers understand only two numbers, 0 and 1, and do all their arithmetic operations in the binary mode. Many electrical and electronic devices have two states: they are either off or on. A light switch is a familiar example, as are vacuum tubes and transistors. Because computers have been a major application for integrated circuits from their beginning, digital integrated circuits have become commonplace. It has thus become easy to design electronic systems that use digital language to control their functions and to communicate with other systems.

A major advantage in using digital methods is that the accuracy of a stream of digital signals can be verified, and, if necessary, errors can be corrected. In contrast, signals that vary in proportion to, say, the sound of an orchestra can be corrupted by "noise," which once present cannot be removed. An example is the sound from a conventional phonograph record, which always contains some extraneous sound from the surface of the recording groove even when the record is new. The noise becomes more pronounced with wear. Contrast this with the sound from a digital compact disc recording. No sound is heard that was not present in the recording studio. The disc and the player contain error-correcting features that remove any incorrect pulses (perhaps arising from dust on the disc) from the information as it is read from the disc.

As electronic systems become more complex, it is essential that errors produced by noise be removed; otherwise, the systems may malfunction. Many electronic systems are required to operate in electrically noisy environments, such as in an automobile. The only practical way to assure immunity from noise is to make such a system operate digitally. That alone may be insufficient, since error-correcting procedures have limits. In principle, it is possible to correct for any arbitrary number of errors, but in practice this may not be possible. The amount of extra information that must be handled to correct for large rates of error reduces the capacity of the system to handle the desired information, and so trade-offs are necessary.

A consequence of the veritable explosion in the number and kinds of electronic systems has been a sharp growth in the electrical noise level of the environment. Any electrical system generates some noise, and all electronic systems are to some degree susceptible to disturbance from noise. The noise may be conducted along wires connected to the system, or it may be radiated through the air. Care is necessary in the design of systems to limit the amount of noise that is generated and to shield the system properly to protect it from external noise sources.

SUPERCOMPUTER

Cray, Seymour R. was the American electronics engineer who was the pre-eminent designer of the large, high-speed computers known as supercomputers.

Cray graduated from the University of Minnesota in 1950 with a bachelor's degree in electrical engineering. He began his career as a computer scientist working on UNIVAC I, a landmark first-generation electronic digital computer that became the first commercially available computer. In 1957 Cray helped found Control Data Corp., which became a major computer manufacturer. There Cray designed the CDC 6600 and the CDC 7600, large-scale computers notable for their high processing speeds.

In 1972 Cray left Control Data to found his own firm, Cray Research Inc., with the intention of building the fastest computers in the world. This was largely realized through his innovative design of multiprocessor computers, which allowed simultaneous (parallel) processing. His company's first supercomputer, the Cray-1, which came out in 1976, could perform 240,000,000 calculations per second. It was used for large-scale scientific applications, such as simulating complex physical phenomena, and was sold to government and university laboratories. Further supercomputers followed, each with increased computing speed: the Cray 1-M and the Cray X-MP. Cray resigned as chairman of his growing firm in 1981 and became an independent contractor to the company, designing ever-faster machines at his laboratory in Chippewa Falls. In 1985 the Cray-2 was introduced to the market; this machine, which was cooled by Fluorinert, could perform 1,200,000,000 calculations per second. The Cray Y-MP, introduced in 1988, was capable of 2,670,000,000 calculations per second. In 1989 Cray founded the Cray Computer Corporation. However, as microprocessor technology advanced and the demand for supercomputers fell in the post-Cold War era, Cray Computers filed for bankruptcy in 1995.

COMPUTER PROGRAM

This is the detailed plan or procedure for solving a problem with a computer; more specifically, an unambiguous, ordered sequence of computational instructions necessary to achieve such a solution. The distinction between computer programs and equipment is often made by referring to the former as software and the latter as hardware.

Programs stored in the memory of a computer enable the computer to perform a variety of tasks in sequence or even intermittently. The idea of an internally stored program was introduced in the late 1940s by the Hungarian-born mathematician John von Neumann. The first digital computer designed with internal programming capacity was the EDVAC (acronym for Electronic Discrete Variable Automatic Computer), constructed in 1949.

A program is prepared by first formulating a task and then expressing it in an appropriate computer language, presumably one suited to the application. The specification thus rendered is translated, commonly in several stages, into a coded program directly executable by the computer on which the task is to be run. The coded program is said to be in machine language, while languages suitable for original formulation are called problem-oriented languages. A wide array of problem-oriented languages has been developed, some of the principal ones being COBOL (Common Business-Oriented Language), FORTRAN (Formula Translation), BASIC (Beginner's All-Purpose Symbolic Instruction Code), and Pascal.

Computers are supplied with various programs designed primarily to assist the user to run jobs or optimize system performance. This collection of programs, called the operating system, is as important to the operation of a computer system as its hardware.

Current technology makes it possible to build in some operating characteristics as fixed programs (introduced by customer orders) into a computer's central processing unit at the time of manufacture. Relative to user programs, the operating system may be in control during execution, as when a time-sharing monitor suspends one program and activates another, or at the time a user program is initiated or terminated, as when a scheduling program determines which user program is to be executed next.

Certain operating-system programs, however, may operate as independent units to facilitate the programming process. These include translators (either assemblers or compilers), which transform an entire program from one language to another; interpreters, which execute a program sequentially, translating at each step; and debuggers, which execute a program piecemeal and monitor various circumstances, enabling the programmer to check whether the operation of the program is correct or not.

ARCHITECTURE

Architecture deals with both the design of computer components (hardware) and the creation of operating systems (software) to control the computer. Although designing and building computers is often considered the province of computer engineering, in practice there exists considerable overlap with computer science.

BASIC COMPUTER COMPONENTS

A digital computer typically consists of a control unit, an arithmetic-logic unit, a memory unit, and input/output units.

The arithmetic-logic unit (ALU) performs simple addition, subtraction, multiplication, division, and logic operations - such as OR and AND. The main computer memory, usually high-speed random-access memory (RAM), stores instructions and data. The control unit fetches data and instructions from memory and effects the operations of the ALU. The control unit and ALU usually are referred to as a processor, or central processing unit (CPU). The operational speed of the CPU primarily determines the speed of the computer as a whole. The basic operation of the CPU is analogous to a computation carried out by a person using an arithmetic calculator, as illustrated in the figure

The control unit corresponds to the human brain and the memory to a notebook that stores the program, initial data, and intermediate and final computational results. In the case of an electronic computer, the CPU and fast memories are realized with transistor circuits.

I/O units, or devices, are commonly referred to as computer peripherals and consist of input units (such as keyboards and optical scanners) for feeding instructions and data into the computer and output units (such as printers and monitors) for displaying results.

In addition to RAM, a computer usually contains some slower, but larger and permanent, secondary memory storage. Almost all computers contain a magnetic storage device known as a hard disk, as well as a disk drive to read from or write to removable magnetic media known as floppy disks. Various optical and magnetic-optical hybrid removable storage media are also quite common, such as CD-ROMs (compact disc read-only memory) and DVD-ROMs (digital video [or versatile] disc read-only memory).

Computers also often contain a cache - a small, extremely fast (compared to RAM) memory unit that can be used to store information that will be urgently or frequently needed. Current research includes cache design and algorithms that can predict what data is likely to be needed next and preload it into the cache for improved performance.

FILE STORAGE

Computers have been used since the 1950s for the storage and processing of data. An important point to note is that the main memory of a computer provides only temporary storage; any data stored in main memory is lost when the power is turned off. For the permanent storage of data, one must turn to auxiliary storage, primarily magnetic and optical media such as tapes, disks, and CDs. Data is stored on such media but must be read into main memory for processing.

A major goal of information-system designers has been to develop software to locate specific data on auxiliary storage and read it efficiently into main memory for processing. The underlying structure of an information system is a set of files stored permanently on some secondary storage device. The software that comprises a file management system supports the logical breakdown of a file into records. Each record describes some thing (or entity) and consists of a number of fields, where each field gives the value of some property (or attribute) of the entity. A simple file of records is adequate for uncomplicated business data, such as an inventory of a grocery store or a collection of customer accounts.

Early file systems were always sequential, meaning that the successive records had to be processed in the order in which they were stored, starting from the beginning and proceeding down to the end. This file structure was appropriate and was in fact the only one possible when files were stored solely on large reels of magnetic tape and skipping around to access random data was not feasible. Sequential files are generally stored in some sorted order (e.g., alphabetic) for printing of reports (e.g., a telephone directory) and for efficient processing of batches of transactions. Banking transactions (deposits and withdrawals), for instance, might be sorted in the same order as the accounts file, so that as each transaction is read the system need only scan ahead (never backward) to find the accounts record to which it applies.

When so-called direct-access storage devices (DASDs; primarily magnetic disks) were developed, it became possible to access a random data block on the disk. (A data block is the unit of transfer between main memory and auxiliary storage and usually consists of several records.) Files can then be indexed so that an arbitrary record can be located and fetched (loaded into the main memory). An index of a file is much like an index of a book; it consists of a listing of identifiers that distinguish the records (e.g., names might be used to identify personnel records), along with the records' locations.

Since indexes might be long, they are usually structured in some hierarchical fashion and are navigated by using pointers, which are identifiers that contain the address (location in memory) of some item. The top level of an index, for example, might contain locations of (point to) indexes to items beginning with the letters, etc. The index itself may contain not locations of data items but pointers to indexes of items beginning with the letters, and so on. Reaching the final pointer to the desired record by traversing such a treelike structure is quite rapid. File systems making use of indexes can be either purely indexed, in which case the records need be in no particular order and every individual record must have an index entry that points to the record's location, or they can be "indexed-sequential." In this case a sort order of the records as well as of the indexes is maintained, and index entries need only give the location of a block of sequentially ordered records.

Searching for a particular record in a file is aided by maintaining secondary indexes on arbitrary attributes as well as by maintaining a primary index on the same attribute on which the file is sorted. For example, a personnel file may be sorted on (and maintain a primary index on) employee identification numbers, but it might also maintain indexes on names and departments. An indexed-sequential file system supports not only file search and manipulation commands of both a sequential and index-based nature but also the automatic creation of indexes.

FORMULATING A DIAGNOSIS

The process of formulating a diagnosis is called clinical decision making. The clinician uses the information gathered from the history and physical examination to develop a list of possible causes of the disorder, called the differential diagnosis. The clinician then decides what tests to order to help refine the list or identify the specific disease responsible for the patient's complaints. During this process, some possible diseases (hypotheses) will be discarded and new ones added as tests either confirm or deny the possibility that a given disease is present. The list is refined until the physician feels justified in moving forward to treatment. Even after treatment is begun, the list of possible diagnoses may be revised further if the patient does not progress as expected.

An algorithm is a sequence of alternate steps that can be taken to solve problems - a decision tree. Starting with a chief complaint or key clue, the physician moves along this decision tree, directed one of two ways by each new piece of information, and eliminates diagnoses. If the wrong path is taken, the physician returns to a previous branching point and follows the other path. Computers can be used to assist in making the diagnosis; however, they lack the intuition of an experienced physician and the nonverbal diagnostic clues obtained during the interview.

HOW INTELLIGENCE IS GATHERED

Good intelligence management must begin with the determination of what needs to be known. Unless precise requirements are set, data will be collected unsystematically and the decision maker left, in the end, without the required information. Once data are collected they must be evaluated and transformed into a usable form (and sometimes stored for future use). Evaluation is essential because of the wide variety of sources, many of them of doubtful reliability. A standardized system is used. Source reliability may be rated A, B, C, etc., down a scale. Information accuracy may likewise be rated 1, 2, 3, etc., with 1 representing confirmed information and 3 denoting a "possibly true" degree of accuracy. Thus the classification of a bit of information as C-3 would mean it came from a fairly reliable source and was possibly true.

With organisational sophistication, refined procedures, and the most advanced technology, intelligence still falls into two categories - the knowable and the unknowable. It is possible to obtain hard intelligence on the number of non-U.S. intercontinental ballistic missiles. But it is not possible to predict, with precision, the political intentions of any foreign leaders.

So vast is the intake of information that intelligence systems have been threatened by inundation. In the years since World War II great efforts have gone into the development of efficient means for cataloguing, storing, and retrieving on demand the gigantic volume of data being amassed. Intelligence agencies have led in developing new indexing and codifying techniques and machinery for the electronic analysis, storage, and location of specific information. Some believe that data collection has been overemphasized at the expense of analysis, but silicon chips and micro-circuitry hold promise for coping with the tidal wave of information.

MODERN CONTROL PRACTICES

There are various cases in industrial control practice in which theoretical automatic control methods are not yet sufficiently advanced to design an automatic control system or completely to predict its effects. This situation is true of the very large, highly interconnected systems such as occur in many industrial plants. In this case, operations research, a mathematical technique for evaluating possible procedures in a given situation, can be of value.

In determining the actual physical control system to be installed in an industrial plant, the instrumentation or control-system engineer has a wide range of possible equipment and methods to use. He may choose to use a set of analogue-type instruments, those that use a continuously varying physical representation of the signal involved - i.e., a current, a voltage, or an air pressure. Devices built to handle such signals, generally called conventional devices, are capable of receiving only one input signal and delivering one output correction. Hence they are usually considered single-loop systems, and the total control system is built up of a collection of such devices. Analogue-type computers are available that can consider several variables at once for more complex control functions. These are very specific in their applications, however, and thus are not commonly used.

With the development of very reliable models in the late 1960s, digital computers quickly became popular elements of industrial-plant-control systems. Computers are applied to industrial control problems in three ways: for supervisory or optimizing control; direct digital control; and hierarchy control.

In supervisory or optimising control the computer operates in an external or secondary capacity, changing the set points in the primary plant-control system either directly or through manual intervention. A chemical process, for example, may take place in a vat the temperature of which is thermostatically regulated. For various reasons, the supervisory control system might intervene to reset the thermostat to a different level. The task of supervisory control is thus to "trim" the plant operation, thereby lowering costs or increasing production. Though the overall potential for gain from supervisory control is sharply limited, a malfunction of the computer cannot adversely affect the plant.

In direct-digital control a single digital computer replaces a group of single-loop analogue controllers. Its greater computational ability makes the substitution possible and also permits the application of more complex advanced-control techniques.

Hierarchy control attempts to apply computers to all the plant-control situations simultaneously. As such, it requires the most advanced computers and most sophisticated automatic-control devices to integrate the plant operation at every level from top-management decision to the movement of a valve.

The advantage offered by the digital computer over the conventional control system described earlier, costs being equal, is that the computer can be programmed readily to carry out a wide variety of separate tasks. In addition, it is fairly easy to change the program so as to carry out a new or revised set of tasks should the nature of the process change or the previously proposed system prove to be inadequate for the proposed task. With digital computers, this can usually be done with no change to the physical equipment of the control system. For the conventional control case, some of the physical hardware apparatus of the control system must be replaced in order to achieve new functions or new implementations of them.

INVENTION OF THE TRANSISTOR

The invention of the transistor in 1947 by John Bardeen, Walter H. Brattain, and William B. Shockley of the Bell research staff provided the first of a series of new devices with remarkable potential for expanding the utility of electronic equipment. Transistors, along with such subsequent developments as integrated circuits, are made of crystalline solid materials called semiconductors, which have electrical properties that can be varied over an extremely wide range by the addition of minuscule quantities of other elements. The electric current in semiconductors is carried by electrons, which have a negative charge, and also by holes, analogous entities that carry a positive charge. The availability of two kinds of charge carriers in semiconductors is a valuable property exploited in many electronic devices made of such materials.

Early transistors were produced using germanium as the semiconductor material, because methods of purifying it to the required degree had been developed during and shortly after World War II. Because the electrical properties of semiconductors are extremely sensitive to the slightest trace of certain other elements, only about one part per billion of such elements can be tolerated in material to be used for making semiconductor devices.

During the late 1950s, research on the purification of silicon succeeded in producing material suitable for semiconductor devices, and new devices made of silicon were manufactured from about 1960. Silicon quickly became the preferred raw material, because it is much more abundant than germanium and thus intrinsically less expensive. In addition, silicon retains its semi-conducting properties at higher temperatures than does germanium. Silicon diodes can be operated at temperatures up to 200° C (392° F), whereas germanium diodes cannot be operated above 85° C. There was one other important property of silicon, not appreciated at the time but crucial to the development of low-cost transistors and integrated circuits: silicon, unlike germanium, forms a tenaciously adhering oxide film with excellent electrical insulating properties when it is heated to high temperatures in the presence of oxygen. This film is utilised as a mask to permit the desired impurities that modify the electrical properties of silicon to be introduced into it during manufacture of semiconductor devices. The mask pattern, formed by a photolithographic process, permits the creation of tiny transistors and other electronic components in the silicon.

By 1960 vacuum tubes were rapidly being supplanted by transistors, because the latter had become less expensive, did not burn out in service, and were much smaller and more reliable. Computers employed hundreds of thousands of transistors each. This fact, together with the need for compact, lightweight electronic missile guidance systems, led to the invention of the integrated circuit (IC) independently by Jack Kilby of Texas Instruments Incorporated in 1958 and by Jean Hoerni and Robert Noyce of Fairchild Semiconductor Corporation in 1959. Kilby is usually credited with having developed the concept of integrating device and circuit elements onto a single silicon chip, while Noyce is given credit for having conceived the method for integrating the separate elements.

Early ICs contained about 10 individual components on a silicon chip 3 millimetres (0.12 inch) square. By 1970 the number was up to 1,000 on a chip the same size at no increase in cost. Late in the following year the first microprocessor was introduced.

MICROPROCESSOR

The microprocessor device contained all the arithmetic, logic, and control circuitry required to perform the functions of a computer's central processing unit. This type of large-scale IC was developed by a team at Intel Corporation, the same company that also introduced the memory integrated circuit in 1971. The stage was now set for the computerization of small electronic equipment.

Until the microprocessor appeared on the scene, computers were essentially discrete pieces of equipment used primarily for data processing and scientific calculations. They ranged in size from minicomputers, comparable in dimensions to a microwave oven, to mainframe systems that took up enough space to fill a large room. The microprocessor enabled computer engineers to develop microcomputers - systems about the size of a lunch box or smaller but with enough computing power to perform many kinds of business, industrial, and scientific tasks. Such systems made it possible to control a host of small instruments or devices (e.g., numerically controlled lathes and one-armed robotic devices for spot welding) by using standard components programmed to do a specific job. The very existence of computer hardware inside such devices is not apparent to the user.

The large demand for microprocessors generated by these initial applications led to high-volume production and a dramatic reduction in cost. This in turn promoted the use of the devices in many other applications - as, for example, in household appliances and automobiles, for which electronic controls had previously been too expensive to consider. Continued advances in IC technology gave rise to very-large-scale integration (VLSI), which substantially increased the circuit density of microprocessors. This technological advance, coupled with further cost reductions stemming from improved manufacturing methods, made feasible the mass production of personal computers for use in schools and homes, as well as in offices.

By the mid-1980s, inexpensive microprocessors had stimulated computerization of an enormous variety of consumer products. Common examples included programmable microwave ovens and thermostats, clothes washers and dryers, self-tuning television sets and self-focusing cameras, videocassette recorders and video games, telephones and answering machines, musical instruments, watches, and security systems. Microelectronics also came to the fore in business, industry, government, and other sectors. Microprocessor-based equipment proliferated, ranging from automatic teller machines and point-of-sale terminals in retail stores to automated factory assembly systems and office workstations.

By mid-1986, memories ICs with a capacity of 262,144 bits (binary digits) were available. Within a short time, circuits of this kind having four times that capacity were being produced. By the mid-1990s, microprocessors capable of handling 32-bit words were common, and 64-bit versions were available. The larger memories and microprocessors contained more than 20 million transistors on a silicon chip less than two centimetres square. In addition, literally tens of thousands of other kinds of ICs for various applications were available, varying in complexity from a few dozen transistors upward.

PERSONAL COMPUTER

(PC), a computer designed for use by only one person at a time. A personal computer is a type of microcomputer--i.e., a small digital computer that uses only one microprocessor. (A microprocessor is a semiconductor chip that contains all the arithmetic, logic, and control circuitry needed to perform the functions of a computer's central processing unit.) A typical personal computer assemblage consists of a central processing unit; primary, or internal, memory, consisting of hard magnetic disks and a disk drive; various input/output devices, including a display screen (cathode-ray tube), keyboard and mouse, modem, and printer; and secondary, or external, memory, usually in the form of floppy disks or CD-ROMs (compact disc read-only memory). Personal computers generally are low-cost machines that can perform most of the functions of larger computers but use software oriented toward easy, single-user applications.

Computers small and inexpensive enough to be purchased by individuals for use in their homes first became feasible in the 1970s, when large-scale integration made it possible to construct a sufficiently powerful microprocessor on a single semiconductor chip. A small firm named MITS made the first personal computer, the Altair. This computer, which used the Intel Corporation's 8080 microprocessor, was developed in 1974. Though the Altair was popular among computer hobbyists, its commercial appeal was limited, since purchasers had to assemble the machine from a kit. The personal computer industry truly began in 1977, when Apple Computer, Inc., founded by Steven P. Jobs and Stephen G. Wozniak, introduced the Apple II, one of the first pre-assembled, mass-produced personal computers. Radio Shack and Commodore Business Machines also introduced personal computers that year. These machines used 8-bit microprocessors (which process information in groups of 8 bits, or binary digits, at a time) and possessed rather limited memory capacity-- i.e., the ability to address a given quantity of data held in memory storage. But because personal computers were much less expensive than mainframes, they could be purchased by individuals, small and medium-sized businesses, and primary and secondary schools. The Apple II received a great boost in popularity when it became the host machine for VisiCalc, the first electronic spreadsheet (computerized accounting program). Other types of application software soon developed for personal computers.

The IBM Corporation, the world's dominant computer maker, did not enter the new market until 1981, when it introduced the IBM Personal Computer, or IBM PC. The IBM PC was only slightly faster than rival machines, but it had about 10 times their memory capacity, and it was backed by IBM's large sales organization. The IBM PC was also the host machine for 1-2-3, an extremely popular spreadsheet introduced by the Lotus Development Corporation in 1982. The IBM PC became the world's most popular personal computer, and both its microprocessor, the Intel 8088, and its operating system, which was adapted from the Microsoft Corporation's MS-DOS system, became industry standards. Rival machines that used Intel microprocessors and MS-DOS became known as "IBM compatibles" if they tried to compete with IBM on the basis of additional computing power or memory and "IBM clones" if they competed simply on the basis of low price.

In 1983 Apple introduced Lisa, a personal computer with a graphical user interface (GUI) to perform routine operations. A GUI is a display format that allows the user to select commands, call up files, start programs, and do other routine tasks by using a device called a mouse to point to pictorial symbols (icons) or lists of menu choices on the screen. This type of format had certain advantages over interfaces in which the user typed text- or character-based commands on a keyboard to perform routine tasks. A GUI's windows, pull-down menus, dialog boxes, and other controlling mechanisms could be used in new programs and applications in a standardized way, so that common tasks were always performed in the same manner. The Lisa's GUI became the basis of Apple's Macintosh personal computer, which was introduced in 1984 and proved extremely successful. The Macintosh was particularly useful for desktop publishing because it could lay out text and graphics on the display screen as they would appear on the printed page.

The Macintosh's graphical interface style was widely adapted by other manufacturers of personal computers and PC software. In 1985 the Microsoft Corporation introduced Microsoft Windows, a graphical user interface that gave MS-DOS-based computers many of the same capabilities of the Macintosh. Windows became the dominant operating environment for personal computers.

These advances in software and operating systems were matched by the development of microprocessors containing ever-greater numbers of circuits, with resulting increases in the processing speed and power of personal computers. The Intel 80386 32-bit microprocessor (introduced 1985) gave the Compaq Computer Corporation's Compaq 386 (introduced 1986) and IBM's PS/2 family of computers (introduced 1987) greater speed and memory capacity. Apple's Mac II computer family made equivalent advances with microprocessors made by the Motorola Corporation. The memory capacity of personal computers had increased from 64 kilobytes (64,000 characters) in the late 1970s to 100 megabytes (100 million characters) by the early '90s.

By 1990 some personal computers had become small enough to be completely portable; they included laptop computers, which could rest in one's lap; notebook computers, which were about the size of a notebook; and pocket, or palm-sized, computers, which could be held in one's hand. At the high end of the PC market, multimedia personal computers equipped with CD-ROM players and digital sound systems allowed users to handle animated images and sound (in addition to text and still images) that were stored on high-capacity CD-ROMs. Personal computers were increasingly interconnected with each other and with larger computers in networks for the purpose of gathering, sending, and sharing information electronically. The uses of personal computers continued to multiply as the machines became more powerful and their application software proliferated. By 1997 about 40 percent of all households in the United States owned a personal computer.

COMPAQ COMPUTER CORPORATION

This is the American computer manufacturer that started as the first maker of IBM-compatible portable computers and quickly grew into the world's best-selling personal computer brand. Headquarters are in Houston, Texas.

Compaq was founded in 1982 by Joseph R. ("Rod") Canion, James M. Harris, and William H. Murto, all former employees of Texas Instruments, Incorporated, for the purpose of building a portable computer that could use all of the software and peripheral devices (monitors, printers, modems) created for the IBM Personal Computer (PC). In 1983, its first full year of production and the year Compaq became a publicly traded corporation; the company shipped 53,000 portable PCs for more than $111 million in revenues--at the time the most by any first-year company in U.S. business history. This would not be Compaq's only business record. It reached the list of Fortune 500 companies (1986) faster than any organization before or since--less than four years after its founding. It was also the youngest company to reach $1 billion in annual sales (1987).

To accomplish these and other achievements, Compaq first perfected, then transformed, the IBM PC clone market. (For many years, personal computers built to the IBM design were known as IBM-compatible, or IBM PC clones.) When IBM introduced its PC in 1981, it built a system with an "open architecture"; that is, the company permitted developers to freely add on hardware and software to improve the features and performance of its PCs. Because IBM also used a microprocessor and a computer operating system that could be acquired from the Intel Corporation and the Microsoft Corporation, respectively, rival companies were able to design and build clones that were "100 percent compatible" - i.e., personal computers that could use anything designed for IBM's PCs. Very early in its history, Compaq became known as one of the best producers of IBM compatibles.

Before it could do anything, however, Compaq had to "reverse engineer" technology that was copyrighted by IBM. Unlike traditional engineering, which seeks to invent new ways of doing something, reverse engineering seeks to re-create existing technology as perfectly as possible, including any flaws. In the clone market, most companies focused exclusively on price. Compaq's engineers took a different approach, concentrating on new features, such as portability and better graphics displays as well as performance - and all at prices comparable to IBM's computers.

Another important distinction from other clone vendors was how Compaq sold its computers. While Dell, Gateway, and others used direct marketing - selling via toll-free telephone numbers and later through the Internet - Compaq, like IBM, sold through independent retailers. Unlike IBM, which also sold its products through other methods, Compaq was renowned for never competing with its retail channel of thousands of loyal computer dealers and resellers.

In 1987 IBM, under intense pressure in the fast-growing personal computer market, introduced a new computer, the PS/2, with a bus that was incompatible with the AT-bus design of earlier IBM PCs. (A computer bus is a set of conductors that enable information to be transmitted between computer components, such as printers, modems, and monitors.) Despite having made its fortune by being 100 percent IBM-compatible, Compaq decided to continue building computers with the original AT bus. Company executives calculated that the $80 billion already spent by corporations on IBM-compatible technology would make it difficult for even IBM to force users to a new design. They were correct. IBM's new technology, although praised in the trade press, did not displace its earlier design. In fact, Compaq's opposition increased its visibility as a leader in PC technology, which it used to line up all of the major PC makers behind a new bus design, called EISA (Extended Industry Standard Architecture). In 1989, Compaq brought the first EISA system to market. That same year the company eclipsed Apple Computer, Inc., as the number two supplier of personal computers behind IBM.

In 1991 the worldwide economic recession and the Persian Gulf War hurt Compaq's profits and pummelled its stock price, leading to the ouster of co-founder and chief executive officer Canion. Canion was replaced by Compaq's long-time European sales and marketing leader, Eckhard Pfeiffer, who had been made chief operating officer and heir apparent after the 1990 retirement of Murto, another cofounder. Under Pfeiffer the company laid off 1,700 employees and aggressively cut prices to shore up market share declines, and it also introduced a variety of lower priced portable and desktop computers, servers, and printers. The strategy paid off. By 1992 the company was profitable again; by 1993 it was the number one supplier of portable computers in America; and in 1995 it passed IBM to become the biggest seller of PCs worldwide.

Encouraged by the long economic expansion of the 1990s, Pfeiffer decided that Compaq could compete more broadly with IBM, the Hewlett-Packard Company, and Sun Microsystems, Inc., either by developing its own line of mainframe computers (the powerful, albeit extremely expensive, big brothers of the PC) or by buying an existing mainframe manufacturer. Compaq embarked on the second course. In 1997 it purchased Tandem Computers for approximately $3 billion, and the next year it bought Digital Equipment Corporation for $9.6 billion. At the same time, Pfeiffer switched the company's long-standing retail strategy to a direct-marketing approach in order to withstand growing competitive pressures from Dell and Gateway. Despite these moves, Compaq failed to unseat even the number two computer company, Hewlett-Packard, and it was replaced as the top personal computer maker by Dell. Following a disastrous first financial quarter in 1999, Pfeiffer lost his job. Integrating two giant acquisitions in less than two years had proved difficult; competition from other personal computer makers were cutting profit margins; and Compaq's institution of direct marketing had decimated its retail distributor network.

COMPUTER MUSIC

Perhaps the most important development in electronic music is the use of digital computers. The kinds of computers employed range from large mainframe, general-purpose machines to special-purpose digital circuits expressly designed for musical uses. Musical applications of digital computers can be grouped into five basic categories: data processing and information retrieval, including library applications and abstracting; processing of music notation and music printing; acoustical, theoretical, and musicological research; music composition; and sound synthesis. In all these fields considerable research and experimentation is being carried out, with sound synthesis perhaps being the most widespread and advanced activity. Dramatic illustrations of the growth of this work include the appearance of the periodical Computer Music Journal, the formation of the Computer Music Association, made up of hundreds of members, and the holding each year of the International Computer Music Conference. The 1982 conference dominated the Venice Biennale - one of the major festivals of contemporary music.

RE-ENGINEERING THE BUSINESS

Business Process Re-engineering (BPR) is the strategic application of analysis and change at a departmental or corporate level to deliver business benefits such as cost savings and efficiency gains. Information technology is often applied to BPR projects, but it is not in itself the BPR. It is more accurately the method enabling business change.

Effective re-engineering starts with assessing operations at a corporate, departmental or even functional level. Each of the business processes involved is analysed to see how it works, how it interrelates with other processes, what it achieves and what it costs. The next stage is to investigate whether each process is necessary and how it might be improved. Finally, new processes are developed and implemented so that improvements are made to overall efficiency, with reduced costs and increased productivity. All of this can be achieved without any information technology whatsoever.

However, in most organisations it is likely that IT can be used to help automate certain processes, eliminate others and introduce new ways of working. For these reasons, it is closely associated with re-engineering and the allied area of workflow, which addresses the need to improve the management of the passage of information through an organisation. Software modelling tools can also aid the process of documenting business work flows in order that the processes are comprehensively understood before considering change.

The key benefits of the business process re-engineering are typically the elimination of wasteful or costly processes, improved customer service, better efficiency and higher productivity. However, BPR should not be viewed as the mere automation of existing processes. Effective BPR will eliminate the wasteful elements of the process and then, if it appropriate, apply systems to deliver the automation and better overall efficiency.

Many of the most successful re-engineering projects have involved the introduction of electronic or paperless trading. Banks and building societies have introduced document image processing, where forms and letters are converted to digital images and processes using computers and work flow practices. There is no need to handle paper. Work loads can be balanced and managed so that maximum productivity and responsiveness to customer requirements is achieved.

In the retail and industrial sectors, examination of the processes involved in the manufacturing and supply chains have led to the application of electronic commerce concepts to streamline the supply chain. Concepts such as Electronic Data Interchange (EDI) have been applied to speed up communications between trading partners, effect the rapid payment of invoices, reduce other lead times and eliminate the cost and potential of errors associated with handling and processing huge amounts of paper.

Organisations considering embarking on re-engineering projects are well advised to talk to consultants and solutions providers with widespread experience in business analysis and re-engineering. These are most likely to have the breath of skills to make a holistic assessment of business processes and to deliver cost effective solutions based on the best available practices and technologies. As with so many parts of business life, careful planning and a clear set of objectives are also essential.

END

INDEX OF CONTENTS:

BIBLIOGRAPHY

AL L BOOKS CATALOGUED IN THIS BIBLIOGRAPHY AND AS MENTIONED BELOW ARE
PUBLISHED BY *ANDREAS SOFRONIOU*

I.T. RISK MANAGEMENT, ISBN: 978-1-4467-5653-9
BUSINESS INFORMATION SYSTEMS, CONCEPTS AND EXAMPLES, ISBN: 978-1-4092-
7338-7 & 0952795639
A GUIDE TO INFORMATION TECHNOLOGY, ISBN: 978-1-4092-7608-1 & 0952795647
CHANGE MANAGEMENT, ISBN: 978-1-4457-6114-5
CHANGE MANAGEMENT IN I.T., ISBN: 978-1-4092-7712-5 & 0952725355
CHANGE MANAGEMENT IN SYSTEMS, ISBN: 978-1-4457-1099-0
FRONT-END DESIGN AND DEVELOPMENT FOR SYSTEMS APPLICATIONS ISBN: 978-1-
4092-7588-6 & 0952725347
I.T RISK MANAGEMENT   ISBN: 978-1-4092-7488-9 & 0952725320
THE SIMPLIFIED PROCEDURES FOR I.T. PROJECTS DEVELOPMENT, ISBN: 978-1-4092-
7562-6 & 0952725312
THE SIGMA METHODOLOGY FOR RISK MANAGEMENT IN SYSTEMS DEVELOPMENT, ISBN:
978-1-4092-7690-6 & 095279568X
TRADING ON THE INTERNET IN THE YEAR 2000 AND BEYOND, ISBN: 978-1-4092- 7577
& 0952795671
STRUCTURED SYSTEMS METHODOLOGY ISBN: 978-1-4477-6610-0
SYSTEMS MANAGEMENT, ISBN: 978-1-4710-4907-1, 978-1-4710-4891-3, 978-1-4710-
4903-3
INFORMATION TECHNOLOGY LOGICAL ANALYSIS, ISBN: 978-1-4717-1688-1
I.T. RISKS LOGICAL ANALYSIS, ISBN: 978-1-4717-1957-8
I.T. CHANGES LOGICAL ANALYSIS, ISBN: 978-1-4717-2288-2
LOGICAL ANALYSIS OF SYSTEMS, RISKS , CHANGES, ISBN: 978-1-4717-2294-3
MANAGE THAT I.T. PROJECT, ISBN: 978-1-4717-5304-6
MANAGEMENT OF I.T. CHANGES, RISKS, WORKSHOPS, EPISTEMOLOGY, ISBN: 978-1-
84753-147-6
THE MANAGEMENT OF COMMERCIAL COMPUTING, ISBN: 978-1-4092-7550-3 &
0952795604
PROGRAMME MANAGEMENT WORKSHOP, ISBN: 978-1-4092-7583-1& 0952725371
THE PHILOSOPHICAL CONCEPTS OF MANAGEMENT THROUGH THE AGES, ISBN: 978-1-
4092- 7554-1 & 0952725363
THE MANAGEMENT OF PROJECTS, SYSTEMS, INTERNET, AND RISKS, ISBN: 978-1-4092-
7464-3 & 0952795698
HOW TO CONSTRUCT YOUR RESUMÊ, ISBN: 978-1-4092-7383-7

www.ingramcontent.com/pod-product-compliance
Lightning Source LLC
Chambersburg PA
CBHW061027050326
40689CB00012B/2727